CANDLE MAGIC

CANDLE MAGIC

A Coveted Collection of Spells
Rituals & Magical Paradigms

PHILLIP COOPER

SAMUEL WEISER, INC.

York Beach, Maine

First published in 2000 by
Samuel Weiser, Inc.
Box 612
York Beach, ME 03910-0612
www.weiserbooks.com

Library of Congress Cataloging-in-Publication Data
Cooper, Phillip, 1955-
    Candle magic : a coveted collection of spells, ritual, and magical
    paradigms / Phillip Cooper.
        p. c.m.
    Includes bibliographical references and index.
    ISBN 1-57863-121-1 (pbk. : alk. paper)
    1. Candles and lights—Miscellanea.   2. Magic.   I. Title.
BF1623.C26 C67 2000
133.4'3—dc21   99–059296

MG

Cover design by Ray Rue
Typeset in 11/13 Minion

Printed in the United States of America

07 06 05 04 03 02 01 00
7   6   5   4   3   2   1

The paper used in this publication meets all the minimum
requirements of the American National Standard for Information
Sciences—Permanence of Paper for Printed Library Materials
Z39.48-1992 (R1997).

Contents

Preface

I am often asked: "Where do I start in magic?" As a novice, faced with masses of literature offering many conflicting viewpoints and an equally baffling array of equipment, you may well be excused for shouting "Help!" My answer to this question is that the best place to start is at the beginning, with yourself.

There are two main reasons why people become involved in magic. The first is to fulfill a need for something in which to believe. Religious hellfire and brimstone simply do not appeal. The second is to solve life's problems—lack of money, ill health, or winning a mate. People searching for answers to material problems, however, almost invariably approach magic with the wrong attitude, usually one of desperation. Magic will never work until negative thinking such as this is reversed. Magic is in and of the mind.

Although this book is designed for the complete novice, more experienced practitioners will also find much in the way of new ideas here. I will show you how to save time and money by adapting everyday articles. I will give you information and ideas, and offer advice on many candle-magic paradigms. I intend this book as a source of practical guidance to anyone interested in understanding candle magic, to those who wish to better their lives by adopting ideas that are safe, natural, and, above all, sensible. I will try to help you to help yourself and I will try to tell you what magic in general is really all about.

More than ever before, I believe, there is a need to clear up the misunderstanding and confusion heaped upon magic and to open the door to reality and point people toward their own inherent abilities. I believe that magic belongs to anyone who has a mind to use it. I believe that the magical arts are simple and natural, and a part of our divine inheritance.

No one controls access to power except you. If you wish to know about real power, or wish to solve life's problems, overcome obstacles, and understand who you are and what your capabilities are, magic may be the answer. It offers a natural way to enhance your life. The aim of this book is to help you to do just that.

Introduction

Burning candles in the hope of attaining some secret wish is an old magical practice so deeply ingrained that even the Christian church has accepted it in a modified form. The ancient art of candle magic has suffered greatly over the centuries from a host of personal biases and superstitions. In this book, I will attempt to remove the mystery from this art, giving only genuine and workable techniques. If you have found the subject confusing before or have failed miserably in the past (as many do!), this book will help you understand the truth and provides techniques that *do* work. Instead of trying to appeal to other-worldly entities, or trying to make sense out of planetary hours, I offer an easier approach to candle magic.

This book attempts to remove the practical obstacles of time and opportunity that busy people today who wish to become ardent practitioners of candle magic often encounter. Nowadays the modern practitioner may be a working man or woman in a city, or a busy farmer unable to take the necessary time to collect virgin wax or to rise up at midnight clad in white linen to use a silver sickle to cut three sprays of apple blossom, and so on.

Candle magic is probably the oldest form of ritual magic known. In recent years, it has made something of a comeback—a fitting testimony to its simplicity and long-standing appeal. Candle-magic practitioners succeed because they contact *power*. Far from being difficult, this is the easiest way to approach magic. There is no need for superhuman effort, complex angelic names, or planetary hours or days. All you needed is the simple approach that is the hallmark of true candle magic. This book presents the facts as they really are, and helps you succeed in bringing happiness and fulfillment into your life through the use of natural energies. The accent is on simplicity, common sense, and the use of practical candle-burning rituals to get positive results.

Since we first discovered fire, the flame has been regarded as something sacred. There can be no doubt that ancient people used fire in magical rituals. Even today, the flame is still considered the finest and simplest focus for the awesome power of the mind. This book uncovers the true art of candle magic from its ancient past, and frees it from medieval mediocrity, superstition, and unnecessary complexities.

The book is designed to be easy to understand. Practical rituals are included, together with lots of useful tips and advice. The accent is on simplicity and on getting results without great expense or unnecessary complexity. Many important areas of life are treated here, including healing, the restoration of self-confidence, money, success, peace of mind, and love. There is no doubt that candle magic can be very effective, if you know what you are doing and you understand the basic facts. All these facts are given to you in this refreshing approach to a very old magical procedure.

I will show you how to work successfully with a minimum of equipment, without all the regalia of religious grandeur. You will learn how to understand what you are doing and why you are doing it. In truth, a magical act must work *every* time. Be realistic. If it does not, then there is something inherently wrong. My aim is to show you why things go wrong, how to avoid pitfalls, and how to put matters right. I firmly believe that everyone has power, and that this power is leaking away, out of control. This is what causes problems. By learning and adopting correct magical techniques, you will be able to take control of this power and direct it according to your needs. While it is true that there are no shortcuts and no instant paths to success, it is also true to say that candle magic is not as complicated as it may appear to be at first.

1
LEARNING CORRECT PROCEDURE

One of the greatest problems ever to confront today's would-be magical practitioner is that of trying to discover the difference between false and genuine magical paradigms. You, as a beginner in magic, are faced with confusion, contradiction, and many uncertainties in your search. You will be pleased to know that you are not alone—many others have also had to suffer these problems.

Each year, an increasing number of people turn to magic in the hope that it will solve their problems. Many are disappointed, some give up altogether, assuming that magic either does not work or is for the select few. Before looking at candle magic, it may perhaps help to look at the problems confronting the novice and attempt to reveal the truth about magical practices.

There are literally thousands of books on magic and related subjects. Candle-burning rituals are quite high on the list of paradigms used to achieve some chosen end. You may have read some of these books, only to find that they are confusing and contradictory. Perhaps you were tempted to buy one of the more popular "instant" magic books—the sort telling you that you do not need any experience, knowledge, or even any equipment! You may even have tried some of the many spells, only to find that you failed. Why? What went wrong? The answer is quite simple. You were given the wrong information!

There is only one way to practice magic and that is the *right* way. First, you must understand why magic works. Then you must learn how to make it work. Let's start from the beginning and build a system of magic that conforms to basic, universal truths and, at the same time, conforms to what is best for *you*.

Discovering magic means recognizing the illusory nature of the material world. All valid mystical and magical traditions achieve this through iron discipline and isolation from society. The aim is to shock the mind into awakening to reality, so that real learning may begin. When you have the time, go forth into the wilderness so that you may discover the magic that lives within yourself. And should some officious agent of bureaucracy intrude on your solitude, remember, that, too, is magic. For *Rex Mundi* hates nothing more than the soul he cannot corrupt or buy, and the entrance of his human emissaries indicates that you are close to discovering real magic.

USING UNIVERSAL ENERGY

Whenever you perform a true magical ritual, you are using energy—a rather special kind of energy. The energy that you use is universal—that is, contained in everything. It is also in abundant supply. It can never be exhausted. Imagine it to be like a natural spring that never runs dry. This source is not distant from you, nor is it difficult to contact, no matter what others may say. It is your right to use this energy for whatever purpose you wish, because you have free choice.

THE SUBCONSCIOUS MIND

This incredible part of your mind is in constant contact with life's energies, and it directs these according to your wishes. It does not know about limitations, obstacles, or the word "impossible." So why is it that you cannot make your wishes come true. Why is it that your rituals do not work, if you really have this power? The answer is really quite simple, when you understand how the subconscious mind works.

Your subconscious mind responds to thought. By thought, I mean deliberate thinking aimed at some objective. Everyday, fleeting thoughts are ignored by the subconscious for a very good reason—if every slight thought affected the subconscious, they would all come true! Imagine the confusion this would create! Fortunately, only sustained thought gets through. When it does, the subconscious, like some vast computer, carries out your wish without any further effort on your behalf.

In order to generate the type of thinking that will affect the subconscious, you must believe in what you are trying to achieve. The subconscious will then accept the directions being given and carry them out. This is a major cause of magical failure. As a novice, you hope and wish for success. When you think about it, the words "hope" and "wish" already suggest the possibility of failure. They are indefinite, they imply the word "if." Trying to get your subconscious to accept an "if," is bound to result in failure, because the word "if," either given directly or implied, will not be accepted. Only positive and assertive thoughts count—in other words, *total* belief.

There are other ways to influence the subconscious mind. These involve using the emotions and the imagination. Any worthwhile magical ritual uses all three. The techniques for using belief, emotions, and the imagination will be discussed in great detail throughout this book. For now, it is only important that you remember these points.

The subconscious mind does not know the difference between good and bad. It only acts on the instructions that you give it and carries them out, whatever they may be. If you believe something, it always comes true. Unfortunately, the ability to believe diminishes with age due to acceptance of supposed facts and lack of practice.

Children, especially the very young, willingly accept (believe) just about anything that they see or hear. The danger is that, if these impressions, or values, happen to be wrong or harmful, they will continue to come true throughout the person's life because they have been accepted by the subconscious mind. That is, unless they are changed. Fortunately, most people do change most of their early beliefs and so their lives get better. However, the beliefs that go unchanged still continue to work, inevitably causing problems. Naturally, people then start to blame others, or some intangible, such as fate or karma. Whole religions and philosophies have been built on this kind of inaccurate thinking. The fault lies not with fate, bad luck, or even with God. The real problem lies within your own subconscious mind.

If this sounds simple—it is. The cause of problems lies within you, therefore the solution to the problem is found, not by blaming life or anyone else, but by substituting new and better beliefs for old ones. Moreover, you now know that you have the power to do this. You, therefore, also have the ability to bring success, happiness, and fulfillment into your life. Magic is a science of the mind. Unfortunately, a lot of absurdity and superstition has crept into magic. So we must look at correct magical procedure if we are to avoid further mistakes.

MAGICAL PLACES AND EQUIPMENT

In order to work effective rituals, you will need a place to work. The place need not be elaborate. If you have a spare room, this will work well. If not, you will need to adapt circumstances to suit your situation. The major consideration is one of privacy. You cannot concentrate on a ritual if you are in constant fear of interruption. It is most important, therefore, to ensure that you will not be disturbed during any ritual. A little ingenuity will often suffice, together with some convenient excuse that will be accepted by those likely to interfere.

Within this workplace, you will need some piece of furniture that can serve as an altar. An altar is not a piece of religious equipment. It is simply a worksurface on which you can place candles and other useful items that are needed during the ritual. It may be a simple coffee table, a dressing table, or whatever comes to hand. It is a good idea to cover this with a clean cloth when working, as this helps to change its appearance from the mundane to the magical.

Candles, candle holders, and other equipment are a matter of choice—it is up to you. Do bear in mind that the more thought and consideration you put into the choice of equipment, the better. Do not rush out and buy any item in the hope that it may suffice. Magic does not work in this way. The more you become involved with your magical equipment and the more careful you are in your choice of these items, the better the result will be. Conversely, it does not follow that the sheer cost of some item will enhance its magical power in some way. The real magic lies within you, not in the equipment. No single piece of equipment, including candles, is, in itself, magical. The equipment is only there to act as a focus for your mind. In candle-burning magic, you will eventually want to have, in addition to your place, altar, altar cloth, candles and candle holders, the following items: incense, incense burners, flowers, herbs, ritual oils, talismans, symbols for particular rituals, a notebook. But you don't need to get them all at once.

When you perform a ritual and light a certain candle, you are performing a symbolic act. It is not the candle that attracts power. It is your mind that attracts. The candle is merely an aid.

MAGICAL RITUALS

When you perform a ritual, there is a set procedure you must follow:

1. Think carefully about your intention.
2. Plan the ritual carefully.
3. Before starting, relax and push aside all thoughts of the day.
4. Perform the ritual, and then sustain positive thinking about your intention over a period of time.

These vital points will be covered step by step in subsequent chapters. For now, just bear them in mind. You may notice a great deal of difference between this approach and the techniques advocated in certain ancient *grimoires*. The difference, apart from the obvious, is that these techniques work. They make all the difference between success and failure!

The purpose of any ritual is to bring together all those items that are relevant to the intention of the rite. The intention dictates all. For instance, suppose you are performing a healing ritual. This comes under the rulership of the Sun, so anything that suggests solar energy should be included, such as gold candles and altar cloths, solar incense (frankincense), sunflowers or marigolds, and perhaps an altar symbol such as a hexagram or solar cross. There are, of course, many other items that could be included. Details on these will be given later.

The purpose of using these items is to help focus your mind along a certain channel, in this case, on the energy of the Sun. It is most important that rituals only include those items that are truly in keeping with the nature and intention of the ritual.

Planetary energies are said to rule all aspects of life. In fact, the planets, as such, do not rule anything. This is a complete misconception. The truth of the matter is that everything that exists contains energy. It is possible, therefore, to group these energies under different headings. As a matter of convenience, all things were once grouped together under certain well-defined headings, according to their similarity to the nature of a particular planet. For instance, the metal gold and the color yellow are more in keeping with the idea of the Sun than, say, Jupiter. Similarly, lead and the color black belong to Saturn.

The classification of everyday facts into planetary groups is called the "doctrine of correspondences." This idea has many uses in magical work, so it is essential that you use only those correspondences that are correct. You will find correspondences elsewhere that won't work as well as the ones I use.

SUMMARY

1. Read this chapter many times. Think about the ideas given to you and compare these ideas with those presented elsewhere. Establish the idea firmly in your mind that you have access to unlimited power by using your subconscious mind.

2. Make a list of your beliefs and ask yourself if they are justified. For instance, if you have written, "I believe in a power that is named God," ask yourself what evidence you have that there is a God? Even more to the point, ask yourself what type of god you believe in? Is your god totally beneficial, or does it exhibit the negative qualities of the Old testament Christian version that is still influencing people today? These are extremely important questions that need to be answered. Get to know your beliefs, because they influence your life!

3. Select a Self Candle that will represent you. Do not rush out and buy any old candle. Think about this

very carefully. What shape will it be? What size and what color? Take your time. Do not be influenced by what you may have read elsewhere. It is your decision and you must come to it all by yourself.

Set up your altar and place your Self Candle in the center. Sit down and spend some time relaxing, pushing aside any everyday thoughts (especially worries) until you are quite calm. If you are not used to being relaxed (and most people are not) the following suggestions may be of help.

You relax by "letting go," not by concentrating. Start by breathing slowly and easily, then move your attention to your feet and imagine that they no longer belong to you. They are getting heavier and heavier. Work slowly through your body, until you are completely relaxed. Either technique works, provided you keep up the practice.

Next, relax your mind. This is where most people have problems. The solution is quite easy. When physically relaxed, simply cast your mind over some pleasant scene. This can be imaginary, or it can be a recollection from the past, such as an enjoyable holiday you once had. Relaxing your mind is easy if you remember that all you have to do is distract it from everyday problems. This can be done as described, or you can use other aids, such as music (not so-called popular music, which is designed to bring out the worst in people!). Classical music is valuable, or any type of music written specifically for meditation, relaxation, or yoga.

The use of incense is also strongly recommended, as this helps promote the right state of mind. Use either loose incense, which needs to be burned on charcoal blocks, or incense (joss) sticks.[1] Recipes for making incense can be found later in this book.

---

[1] Joss sticks are the easiest and simplest way of burning incense. *Joss* means "lucky." You can buy it in most metaphysical bookstores or health food stores.

When you are relaxed, strike a match and light your Self Candle. Put aside the matches and think about what you have just done. You have not just lit a candle for the sake of brightening a room. You lit this candle for a purpose, a reason. In magic, everything must have a purpose. Never do anything without a reason, or it may cause problems. Your purpose here is not just to light a candle. It is to open yourself and your temple to magical power, to redirect your thinking and your awareness away from everyday living, to do something with intention, while using an object as a focus of attention. Think about this very carefully. There is a world of difference between just lighting a candle and lighting it for a purpose. This is the beginning of real magic. Sit down somewhere and think about how the flame you have kindled is different, special. It is like no other flame in existence. It was created by you for a reason. The more you think about this, the more effectual this action will become. The more you get involved in it, the greater the result will be.

Add some meaningful words to the rite, words such as, "I now open this temple to the powers of light and attainment." Then light the candle, pause to contemplate it, and then say something like, "I now open myself to light and truth." Sit and think about the lighting of the candle and the words that you have spoken. There is no need to use my words. In fact, it is better to use your own. Think up your own ritual words. Personalize your rituals so that they fit you and your requirements. Be an individual. Create your own rites in your own way. By all means, look at the works of others and learn from them, but do not copy them parrot-fashion, or you run the real risk of selling yourself short. Ideas will occur if you give them a chance, so be patient and determined. Think about this candle. It represents you—not the ordinary you, but the "real you." Do you remember what the real "you" is? Cast your mind over all that has been written so far concerning your subconscious mind and the power that you have at your command.

Next, think about all the things that you need and want. Do not restrict yourself in any way—be completely positive and let your imagination work fully. Remember that, *in truth,* nothing is impossible. All you have to do is instruct your subconscious mind and your intention is bound to come true.

It is very important not to let self-restricting ideas (or beliefs) get in the way. Treat this as an enjoyable exercise at all times. Whenever you come up against any negative thoughts, such as, "I cannot," or, "if only," dismiss them and remember that you *can*. Never let the apparent facts get in the way. As you will see, these so-called facts can be changed.

Keep up this exercise for as long as you like, performing it at least once a day. Not only will you learn a great deal about yourself and life, you will also notice a difference in *you*. Keep up this practice and do not allow other matters, such as "I don't have time today," to get in the way. If you want to change your life and make magic work for you, you must be prepared to make some sacrifice. You must learn persistence and patience.

Having opened a rite, you must always close it. Just as surely as you must have an effective "in," you must also have an equally effective "out." Opening a rite does and should take up some time. Closing one is much easier and quicker, but it is still an essential part of any rite, so you should give this as much thought as possible. At the conclusion of the thinking session, the length of which is entirely up to you and your circumstances, stand up and declare that this is indeed the end of the session. Say something, or at least think something, that clearly indicates that this is the end of the main work and that you now intend to close down and return to normal. You could, for instance, say, "I now declare the work finished. May the benefits flow freely forth into my everyday life."

Once again, you should formulate your own closing statements, then move to the candle and affirm that the temple is to be closed and that you are about to return to everyday living. Gently blow out the candle or extinguish it in some way that is meaningful, then pause to remember that you are not destroying the flame, only returning it to its own inner place, where it will remain ready and waiting to return whenever you have need of it. Then leave the temple. If you wish (and this is perhaps a good idea), keep a notebook and record any important thoughts that have occurred during the rite. Make lists of all the ideas that occur to you. These lists will be the subject for many rituals later on, for they are your intentions. Extinguish the candle and put everything away until the next session.

Naturally, you can add to this list at any time. In fact, it is always a good idea to spend odd moments looking at the things you have and do not have in order to decide what you really want. Knowing what you really want is equivalent to being halfway along the path to actually getting what you want, so think and practice these exercises until you are proficient at them.

2

CIRCLES OF POWER

Magic is a science—the science of using your mind. In fact, any sufficiently advanced form of magic will appear indistinguishable from science. This thought should be kept uppermost in your mind throughout your magical work if you are to avoid the pitfalls that lie between you and success. With this thought in mind, let us now look at the correct way to perform a candle-magic ritual. The best procedure is as follows:

1. Think out your intention first;
2. Plan your ritual;
3. Prepare for your ritual.

These are essential preliminaries. At the chosen time, and with all equipment in place, then

4. Relax;
5. Perform your ritual;
6. Clear everything away.

These six points are all important steps to success. Let us now look at each in detail.

THINK OUT YOUR INTENTION

Numerous rituals fail simply because the intention was not clear in the practitioner's mind. Remember that it is your mind with which you are working. It, therefore, naturally follows that, if your mind is in a state of confusion, you are unlikely to get good results. All doubts, fears, and uncertainties must be dealt with one at a time and replaced with positive thoughts. No matter how long this takes, it is essential that you do it, in order to avoid problems later. Nothing is more distracting than experiencing a battery of worries during a ritual. Think about your intention from all possible angles, root out all fears, and be positive. The end result must be that, when you perform your ritual, you know exactly what you want and are confident of success.

Suppose that your intention is to acquire a new car. You should spend some time thinking about this, gradually getting the image clear in your mind. You should decide on the make, color, and type of vehicle. Will it be a new car or second-hand? Do you need good fuel economy? While you are doing this, certain doubts may come to mind. Don't ignore them, or let them take control. Instead, examine these doubts—you can learn from them.

The SWOT Analysis

The acronym, SWOT, stands for Strengths, Weaknesses, Opportunities, Threats. The SWOT analysis may be useful for studying the situation. This technique identifies as many different opportunities as possible that can be used to influence the desired result. If you indulge in hasty action without assessing the situation, your own weaknesses may lead to problems that you may not envisage at the outset. This analysis can sometimes be useful for examining a situation prior to taking magical action.

Strengths: Look at the strength of your position—material links, inside information concerning your intention, and anything likely to aid your success. Concentrate on the most appropriate variable to nudge the event in your favor.

Weaknesses: Look at the things that could go against you, or the possible weaknesses of your position. Is it really worth it? Do the costs, in terms of time and effort, outweigh the success? Can anything interfere with the materialization of your intention?

Opportunities: Consider the timing. Is there an optimum time to cast the spell or work the ritual? What do you anticipate gaining from this working? Take into account the astrological considerations, phases of the Moon, and planetary aspects.

Threats: What could go wrong and, if it did, how would it affect the situation? How would you cope with the new event and with the negative consequences of your spell or ritual?

If you find that there are many threats and weaknesses to your spell or ritual, it may be wise to reconsider your intention. Consider the circumstances. What is the likely course of events if you do not take action? Divination, such as reading runes or the tarot, may be useful here. Gather information, analyze the situation, evaluate your intention again if necessary, and then act.

Remember every cause has an effect, and every effect has a cause. In magic, substitute the word "thought" for "cause," and you have a major key to power. Sustained thinking causes things to happen. Indeed, what is magic other than a way of sustaining a thought pattern in order to obtain a desired result? It is, therefore, vital that, before you embark on some magical action, you think carefully about the effect that it may have. Quite often, the novice surges forth with great enthusiasm, performs the ritual, gets the desired result, and then wishes that he or she had not bothered, because all the effects had not been considered.

Take, for instance, the idea of winning millions in the lottery. Sounds like a good idea! Now, really think about this and the dramatic side effects this would inevitably have. Your entire lifestyle would change. You may have to think of changing your home, employing accountants to look after your newfound wealth, hiring security guards to protect you against thieves, coping with begging letters and all those "hangers on." A simple cause can produce many effects, some of which may be undesirable.

The golden rule is, therefore, to endeavor to consider all the facts before you act. Naturally, it is not possible to foresee every eventuality. This takes a lot of skill and a rare quality known as wisdom. The more you apply the idea of "look before you leap," however, the better the outcome will be in a more general sense.

PLAN YOUR RITUAL

Your intention will dictate the nature of your ritual and the equipment you will use. Some time should be spent thinking carefully about this. For instance, how many candles will you use? What color will these be? Which incense will you use? What is the best time for your ritual? Every last detail must be sorted out satisfactorily. It is a good idea to write a list that can then be used as a guide later on.

PREPARE FOR YOUR RITUAL

Use your checklist to lay out all your equipment and candles, so that, when you are ready to start, everything is in its place.

Your sole intention, up to now, has been to remove the chances of distractions and mistakes. Get into the habit of being meticulous in both thought and action. Cultivate positive thinking, together with good habits, and always bear in mind that your pre-ritual work largely dictates the outcome.

LEARN TO RELAX

No ritual is ever likely to succeed if you are in a state of turmoil, and your mind is cluttered with everyday thoughts. It is vital that you spend some time relaxing and pushing aside all thoughts that are not connected with the intention of your rite. You may do this either in your place of work (now referred to as your temple), or any place that is quiet and free from distractions. Incense and soft music will be of great value in helping you unwind. When this is achieved, gradually concentrate on the intention of the ritual and build up positive thoughts concerning it. Start by considering the ideas given later on universal energy and the power within your subconscious mind (see page 18).

PERFORM YOUR RITUAL

Having established what you are about to do, how you are going to do it and why you are performing the ritual, the actual rite should be a relaxed and happy event, free from negative thoughts and problems arising from lack of planning. If something does go wrong, don't panic. Take careful stock of the situation and see if it is worth carrying on. Don't let fear take over. Stay calm and gradually come to a decision. If possible, carry on, unless it really is impossible, in which case, close down the ritual (see below) and perform the rite another day. If all goes well, close down as normal.

CLEAR AWAY EVERYTHING

If you are using a temporary altar, you will need to clear everything away. There are two main reasons for this. First, it is never a good idea to leave things lying around for others to see. The act of clearing away also helps to bring matters "down to earth." The purpose of a ritual is simply to focus your mind on your intention and on the power you want to use. Let us now look at this power.

YOU AND YOUR SUBCONSCIOUS

Everything in creation contains energy. It is this energy, or power, that you use to attract more desirable circumstances and physical objects into your life. The instrument by which you do this is the subconscious mind. This involves a process in which you, your subconscious, and your beliefs make contact with universal energy.

You as a human being, are far more powerful than you realize, because you have the ability to create by using energy and directing it with your subconscious mind. At first glance, this may seem to be a massive overestimation or a flight of fancy. Let me assure you that it is true. Your ability to create is vast and unlimited. In addition, you use this power all the time, without being aware of it. The law, in this respect, is that you either control this power consciously and direct it toward things that are desirable, or the power will continue to work unchecked, possibly doing harm to you and others. Magic is the art of understanding and controlling this power.

Your subconscious mind is "the God within," or your *personal power center*. Not only does it direct power on your behalf, it also responds to direct instructions, whatever these may be, and provides answers to questions. *Never* underestimate the sheer power and vast scope inherent in this part of you.

When you are dealing with magic, you are dealing with the science of instructing the subconscious mind and using its vast potential. Always keep this idea uppermost in your mind, or your magical work may well fall into error through superstition and other unworkable paradigms.

YOUR BELIEFS

The subconscious mind will only act on an instruction if it is given in a specific way. That way is through belief. According to the laws of the cosmos, anything that is believed is bound to come true. This is entirely due to the workings of the subconscious, not to the more popular idea of intervention by "beings" external to your self. "Do gods really exist?" This is a question I have heard many times. In fact, they do exist in the form of personalized energies. This is what makes us think they are real.

Most people think that believing is difficult, because they take the wrong approach. Belief is not something you have to force into existence. On the contrary, all you have to do is simply accept that something is true and hold to this belief despite the so-called facts. In magic, you must never let the supposed facts dictate how you think and act. These facts are there to be altered, if you wish it so. Magic is concerned with altering these facts so they become more favorable.

Creative Thinking

You can influence your subconscious mind by establishing a belief on which it can act. There are many ways you can do this. Some are outside the scope of this book. Other, more applicable, magical paradigms will be discussed in full. The key is to use thought to establish a belief pattern that is subsequently acted on without any further effort on your part. It is, however, the *quality* of thought that matters. Everyday thinking has no effect.

Your subconscious mind is only receptive to sustained thought, backed up by feeling and the imagination. In addition, your subconscious mind does not understand the English language (or any other system of spoken words). It only understands symbols given to it by the imagination. The use of symbols will be discussed in a moment; for now, let's look at the right way to perform a magical ritual.

RITUAL INVOLVEMENT

The more you put in your own rituals, the more you get out of them. By this, I do not necessarily mean expense. To be truthful, a 50¢ candle will be just as effective as one that costs you $5.00. What really matters is the type of relationship that exists between you and the object of attention. You can either have a piece of equipment that has been chosen using superstition or little thought, or you can have something that has been carefully thought about and, as a result, means something to you. The "intent" in your ritual will be obvious.

Words, as such, mean little to your subconscious mind. Only thoughts count. There is a world of difference between saying words and meaning what you say! Suppose you use the words, "I desire health," in a ritual. You can simply speak the words, or you can speak them with conviction, with authority, and with assertion. In other words, you indicate that you confidently believe in what you are saying. The difference between this approach and pleas for help that are advocated elsewhere is clear. Language is founded on a fundamental misconception of reality. Expecting that anyone can explain magic in words is like asking an artist to reproduce a Caravaggio with a yard broom and a bucket of tar. Language sees the world as objects and materials in space, whereas it is really illusion caused by a single living process. The energy causing the process and creating the phantasmagoria you mistake for reality is the power that is harnessed to accomplish practical magic.

When performing a ritual, you are asking something of life because you are entitled to—it is your right. Universal energy is there to be used in any way you wish, although a wise person will consider all aspects before performing a ritual for some end result. You can have whatever you want, if you ask in the right way. You should always bear in mind, however, that you are responsible for whatever you create. It makes good sense to think carefully before you set power in motion.

Remember that, although there is no doubt that there is intelligence behind life's energies, this God (or whatever you care to name it) does not pass judgment on your motives and actions, nor does it ever seek to control you. It is utterly against all cosmic law to presume that you are condemned or restricted by any god, spirit, or other supposed external force or entity. The truth is that you have total free choice in the way you use the energies that life freely supplies. If you wish to destroy yourself or others, you can choose to do this (many have!). If you choose to live in wealth, happiness, and abundance, the same forces are at your disposal. God, as such, will not stop you from doing this. On the other hand, other people may not like what you are doing to them and may, therefore, exert their right to stop you from being a nuisance.

It is very important to realize the truth of all this and accept the conclusion that, as a result of free choice, you have to behave in a responsible manner. Before you decide on a course of action, stop and consider it carefully, especially if your desire concerns other people. Decide what you want, by all means, but consider the likely implications as well. Consider them, I said. Don't worry about them!

The Right Way

Remember that magic is a science and, although it uses natural energies in perfectly natural ways, it does require careful study and the understanding of certain laws and principles. Magic works, provided that you treat the subject seriously, apply simple common sense, and don't "dabble" as though magic were some sort of part-time hobby. One of the greatest magical rules is:

$$Input = Output$$

The more you put in, the more you get out. There are no shortcuts or "instant" formulas for success. It all comes down to effort. If you want results, you will have to work for them. The quality of your input is also important. Sane and reliable techniques get good results. Anything else will bring self-delusion and ultimate failure. The choice is yours, but it's worth the effort to acquire knowledge and power that can elevate you above the rest.

Symbolism

Having established that you need to exert positive thinking and believe in what you are doing, let's look at another key to correct magical work—symbolism. As stated, the subconscious mind does not deal in words. It responds only to thought, or, to be more correct, to a type of thought that involves the imagination. You have doubtless heard of visualization. This, however, is not always a desirable way to do things, particularly if you are the kind of person who has difficulty sustaining pictures in your mind. If you can do this easily, well and good. If not, do not spend your valuable time straining to perform visualization exercises. It will be quite pointless. Instead, use the far more natural technique of imagining.

Let me illustrate how the imagination works. This exercise is important, so don't pass it by. All that I want you to do is to describe a five-dollar bill or some comparable bill in whatever your native currency is. Do not look at it. Take your time and think about it slowly and deliberately. I am not as much interested in the description you give as the way in which you arrive at that description. Notice how you arrived at your description. You thought about the bill and formed pictures in your mind. You used your imagination. You also found out that this is perfectly natural and was not in any way difficult. The key is *thinking in pictures.*

Thinking in Pictures
Think about your desire almost as if this were a pleasant game, just as you might think back to some happy memory from the past. Spend as long as you like on this before continuing. Here again, you are using your imagination to create pictures based on the thoughts held in your mind. You can now see the difference between this type of thinking and ordinary, everyday thought. You can now also realize that thinking in imaginary pictures can activate the subconscious mind, which, in turn, will direct power on your behalf in order to achieve that upon which you have been concentrating. Before this can happen, however, you must add one more ingredient—creative thinking.

Thinking about something in the imagination stimulates the subconscious mind into a condition of readiness. It is unlikely, however, that the subconscious will act on these pictures until you give it a positive inclination to do so. You can do this simply by adding desire and a positive assertion that you really do want the things that you are seeing in your imagination. The whole process is like a combination lock—unless you use the right numbers, nothing happens. So it is with creative thinking. These are the essential elements of the process.

> You must have some goal or end product in mind;
> You must think about that goal in your imagination;
> You must actively desire to have or achieve this goal;
> The whole process must be *positive.*

Creative thinking, by itself, will cause things to manifest in your life. This is the essence of mind-power books. If practiced carefully, this process is bound to result in success. It is the last item on this list that causes problems. It is simply of no use to imagine that which you desire while at the same time telling yourself that you cannot have it. All negative ideas have to be ignored during these sessions. You have to believe that you are bound to succeed. This requires careful practice. There are numerous ways to do this, but the easiest by far is to drive away negative thoughts by using the imagination in two ways. First, think about your desire in expectation or anticipation. Imagine that it is actually on its way. Then spend some time imagining that you already have the thing you desire. This is not a children's game or some pointless pursuit. It is a scientific way of guaranteeing that you will get whatever you desire. Creative thinking works because you are presenting your subconscious mind with pictures backed up by positive instructions. Those pictures are, in actual fact, symbols, in that they represent an idea. There are many types of symbols, but without going into too much detail, you need only concern yourself with two kinds: the imaginary pictures already discussed, and abstract symbols.

There are many types of abstract symbols that can be used in magical work. You need only concern yourself with the master symbol—the Encircled Cross (see figure 1). This powerful symbol has many uses, the main one being that it can act as a key to subconscious power. This symbol defines the magic circle in which you must work in order to be fully effective. Forget all about those scenes in which witches stand inside a magic circle repelling demons and other astral "nasties." This is absurd and those who still insist on performing rituals in this manner are to be pitied. They know nothing of real magic.

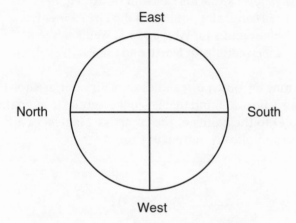

Figure 1. *The Encircled Cross.*
In constructing the Encircled Cross, magical East is
always in front of you and need not correspond
to the actual compass point.

A magical ritual brings (or should bring) together all those elements that are needed to influence the subconscious mind. The essential ingredients are creative thinking, equipment relevant to the intention and the nature of the energy being used, and, of course, symbolism. Apart from the use of abstract symbols, all meaningful pieces of equipment should also be symbolic. In other words, they must represent some idea. An example of this is your Self Candle, which represents you and is therefore symbolic. This will be explored in greater detail later in the book.

Your First Ritual

For this you will need your Self Candle and four standard ¾-inch candles that represent the four gateways of power. These are

> 1 yellow candle for East and the Air element
> 1 red candle for South and the Fire element
> 1 blue candle for West and the Water element
> 1 green candle for North and the Earth element

You may lay out your candles on your altar as shown in figure 2. Bear in mind that it is not essential to align these candles to the points of the compass. Magical east is always symbolically in front of you.

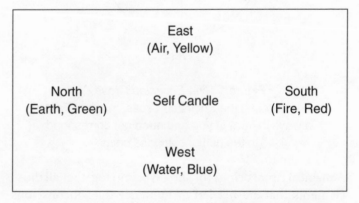

Figure 2.   *Element candles at the gateway of power.*

The purpose of this ritual is to familiarize yourself with basic magical procedure and build a symbolic base on which to develop your magical abilities. Start by laying out the equipment, then spend some time relaxing your body and mind until you are quite calm. Do not rush! When you are ready, open the ritual.

Your opening and closing formulas are vital to the success of your ritual. They act as a positive On/off switch that the subconscious mind can recognize and on which it can act. They give you control, just as a switch allows you to turn electricity on and off.

This ritual is done in the imagination. All you have to do is imagine that there is a sturdy door in front of you that bears the Encircled Cross symbol. Imagine that the door opens and that you are passing through it. Next, light your Self Candle as a symbolic representation of your inner power (your subconscious mind). Contemplate this and the ideas given to you in this chapter for a while. Now imagine that you are standing in the center of a huge Encircled Cross traced out in shining light. Do not strain to see this—simply imagine that it is there. A useful aid to concentration is to focus on this using a short phrase that acts as a command, such as, "Circle of Cosmos—arise." Let this build up in your imagination. This is the beginning of the true magic circle that you will develop later on.

Next, bring in the idea of the four elements. You need not understand the complexity of the fourfold system of power that exists within everything. All that matters is that you erect a symbolic representation of it in your imagination. To do this, use your imagination to see another doorway right in front of you. This door is colored yellow and represents the power of the Air element. See this open, letting bright yellow light into your temple. Now light the yellow candle, which, of course, is a symbol of this power.

Now imagine a red doorway. This is the doorway of the Fire element. See this open, allowing red light to enter the temple. Light the red candle to signify this power. Then imagine a blue doorway. This is the door of the Water element. See this open, allowing blue light into the temple. Light the blue candle to signify this. Finally, see a green door that equates to the Earth element. Open this and allow green light to enter the temple, finally lighting the green candle to represent this.

Your temple has now been opened symbolically and is ready for the main magical work. I would suggest that you burn some general incense or joss sticks at this point and, once again, consider your desires in the light of what has been written in this chapter. In other words, use creative thinking. Spend as long as you like on this, remembering that "input = output" (or, put another way, "practice makes perfect"). The more you practice this basic procedure, the better, because you are stimulating your subconscious mind into action by using a symbol pattern it understands. When finished, you must perform the closing formula. This is quite simple, as it is simply the reverse of the opening. Start by seeing the eastern doorway (Air) close firmly, then extinguish the yellow candle. Do the same with the southern (red), western (blue), and northern (green) doorways, in that order. All that remains to be done now is to extinguish your Self Candle and return to normal consciousness. It is important to reverse the momentum of the ritual by using another command phrase, such as "Circle of Cosmos—depart." Now see yourself going back through the original door through which you came. See this door close firmly. The closing is complete.

Practice this often, preferably once a day, until you feel proficient. Then move on to the next chapter, in which you will develop these ideas further.

3
THE MAGIC SPHERE

In the latter half of the 20th century, our awareness is expanding and our technology is advancing at an enormous rate. Science is helping sweep away the fetters of religious dogma, yet the great science of magic is a shambles and its present-day credibility extremely low. The problem lies in the lack of knowledge about basic magical technique. There is little cohesive information available to let people know how magic works. To work magic, you have to be trained; you need to know the basics the same way you would for any other subject. For instance, you would not dream of building a house without a plan, or going on a long journey without a map. You could, but imagine the sheer waste of time and effort, not to mention the cost. It is exactly the same with magic. You must have a plan of action in addition to knowledge of the basic techniques.

THE ENCIRCLED CROSS

Symbols are the keys that unlock the doorway to power, and so it is to symbolism that you must turn if you are to discover a realistic plan that can lead to magical success. The master symbol is the Encircled Cross (see figure 1, page 25). Like the circuit diagram of an electrical engineer, this symbol is a plan of power to those who know how to use it. Let us examine this symbol in some detail to see how this works.

THE CENTER

The central point of the cross represents the power of your subconscious mind, or the inner self. There is nothing mysterious about the inner self; sometimes it is called the "holy guardian angel" or "the true self." It is simply that part of you that mediates power and is connected to everything that exists or has existed. It is perfectly valid to view the subconscious mind in this way—for example, to use a personalized image—another type of symbol. Things go wrong when this image becomes too far removed and appears untouchable, as in the case of the Christian images. Here, the image has been allowed to take on a sinister and oppressive nature, with the result that power is now restricted by belief. As you now know, whatever you believe comes true. That is why millions of Christian thinkers live in fear. How much better to build an image of a totally beneficent God who will grant you whatever you wish and will answer all your questions. Your idea (image) of God determines what you get, because creation (God) can only supply those things that are in keeping with your beliefs. Exactly the same thing is likely to happen with any other personalized images, be these gods, angels, demons, spirits, or, of course, your inner self.

The point is purely one of using only beneficial images that are free from self-restricting concepts. How foolish and self-defeating to think of things as beyond your ability to understand them, or as elevated and therefore unreachable, or as more powerful than you, so that you must grovel, sacrifice, or appease in order to gain favor. You must not believe that things have the power to control you. This is, perhaps, the most dangerous misconception of all. Unfortunately, it is also the most prevalent.

The power of the center is yours. It is not distant, nor is it difficult to contact. You most certainly do not have to degrade yourself in order to use it because it is part of you. Treat your central subconscious power realistically, by adopting positive and essentially beneficial beliefs. By doing this, you open up the channels of power rather than blocking them up with unfounded beliefs and superstition.

The Cross

This ancient symbol has nothing whatsoever to do with the Christian symbol of the crucifix. It is a symbol of power in action, flowing from the center, outward along the four paths that make up the arms of the cross. A reasonable comparison would be to the wires or printed circuits that connect electronic components and allow electricity to flow. Each path of the cross is said to be ruled by an element (Air, Fire, Water, and Earth). These bear little resemblance to their physical counterparts and should be considered more as four different ways of expressing power.

There is no need for a discussion of the complexities of these elements. It is sufficient to recognize that these do exist, albeit on a symbolic level, allowing the subconscious mind to work through these four channels. In short, if you make provision for power to flow through its natural elemental channels, the subconscious mind will respond. It will, of course, do this far better if you acknowledge the elements than if you ignore them.

The Circle

As the central point is the beginning, so the circle is the end and represents completion. Everything created by the center is contained in the circle. All through life, circles are formed, to a greater or lesser extent. You can see this quite easily if you look around you. Circles link together and, at the same time, they exclude anything that is not in keeping with a central theme—anything from close friendships to a witches' coven can exhibit these tendencies. Circles, therefore, both encompass and exclude. This paradigm is used in magic, not as the now-outmoded idea of standing inside a so-called magic circle while resisting hordes of demons, but more scientifically.

The subconscious mind fully understands the inner truths of the circle and it will, therefore, suffice to use this symbolically, in order to get full subconscious cooperation. This will be dealt with shortly. If you keep in mind, however, the fact that the magic circle is not used as a protective device, you will not go far wrong.

The Encircled Cross is a fitting foundation from many points of view, for, not only does the subconscious mind recognize this and respond to it, it also has many mysteries contained within its simple design that make it an admirable subject for meditation. Let us return to a more pragmatic theme—that of using the symbol within the context of ritual.

THE MAGIC SPHERE

In chapter 2, I described the Encircled Cross as a true magic circle in which you can work. I brought in the idea of symbolism through the use of candles. You will now extend this scheme. The Encircled Cross has, up to now, been a flat design and, as such, can still be quite valuable. However, just as you live in a three-dimensional world, so you must now construct a similar symbolic base for magical practice. This leads you to the concept of a three-dimensional magic sphere, rather than the plain two-dimensional circle. Do not be put off by the apparent complexity of the following procedure. It really is quite simple to follow and, with a little patient practice, the results are well worth the additional effort, as you will see.

Stage One

This is simply an exercise in getting to know the procedure, and may be dispensed with when you are fully conversant with the basic technique. Start, as always, by relaxing and clearing your mind of all mundane thoughts. Then imagine a point of bright light inside yourself, at about heart level. See a shaft of light rise upward to some convenient distance (6 to 8 feet), thereby forming the first path and establishing the top of the sphere (see figure 3, page 35). Do the same in downward direction to form the second path and establish the base of the sphere. Now begin to form the arms of the cross by imagining a beam of light proceeding from the center to a similar distance in the direction of magical East, which, of course, lies in front of you. Repeat this with magical South (right), magical West (behind), and finally magical North (left). All that remains to be done is to complete the sphere by adding the triple rings of cosmos.

The first ring starts from the uppermost point. You can imagine this as a ring of light proceeding in a clockwise direction through the southern, base, and northern points, finally returning to top. The second ring also starts at the top, but this time it moves forward through the eastern, base, and western points, and back to top once more. The final circle, the third ring, is the magic circle with which you are familiar. This starts at the eastern point and proceeds, in a clockwise direction, through the southern, western, and northern points and back to East once more. The magic sphere is now complete. To close down this ritual, simply reverse the procedure, finally seeing the central light disappear. Remember that it is not important that you hold a vivid picture of this in your mind or strain to see it. Follow the guidance given on the use of the imagination in chapter 2. Relax and imagine that the sphere is being constructed around you. Your subconscious will understand what you are doing because you are thinking creatively. Children have the gift of imagination and have little or no difficulty living in other worlds. They know how to pretend. There is nothing wrong with pretending, if it is done constructively. Pretend that you are erecting the magic sphere and let go of the restrictions that tell you this is silly.

I assure you that it is not. In fact, you will find this technique advocated in many mind-power books, in which you are advised to act and think as though you actually have the thing you desire. This may be sound psychology, but is it not also pretence in a positive form?

Practice this exercise often before you move on to Stage Two. Do not rush through it. Take your time, until you are familiar with the sphere and its construction. When you are satisfied that you are confident, move on to Stage Two.

Stage Two

In this stage you move into the realms of magical ritual, not only by erecting the symbol, but by using objects to symbolize the sphere, thereby adding impact on subconscious levels. Naturally, you will use candles as your focus of attention. For this ritual, you will need the equipment described in the practical work of Circles of Power (see page 26). These should be laid out as before, and you should relax completely before beginning.

Imagine the inner light becoming brighter and more powerful. Take your time and realize that this symbolizes your subconscious mind in action. Think about this while casting your mind over all that has been written about the subconscious and its potential. Light the central candle that now symbolizes this inner power. In other words, you now have a physical representation of this power, rather than a plain candle. From the flame, imagine that a beam of light is rising upward to form the first path, terminating at the top of the sphere. Similarly, imagine a beam of light traveling down toward the base, thereby forming the second path. The central axis is now complete.

Again, using the flame as the center point, see a beam of light go out toward magical East. Light the yellow candle to symbolize this point. Do exactly the same with the other three arms of the cross, in turn, lighting the appropriate candle each time. Finally, use your imagination to see the magic rings being formed, as in the previous exercise. The magic sphere is now complete.

This entire process is known as opening the temple. It will, with practice, serve to inform your subconscious mind that you wish to work magically. If you view this as a sort of on/off switch, you will have a reasonable idea of its function. Temple opening (and closing) should never be omitted from any magical work if you truly wish to make good progress and, at the same time, avoid problems. You are aiming for control. Magic without control is both pointless and self-defeating. As in previous exercises, closing down is accomplished by reversing the procedure, clearing everything away, and returning to normal.

The temple opening, in effect, puts your subconscious mind into a condition of readiness for whatever is to follow—the actual magical work itself. There is, however, an intermediary step that activates the magic sphere in a very special way. This is not particularly difficult, although it does require some practice. It does not require any additional equipment—it is done entirely in the imagination.

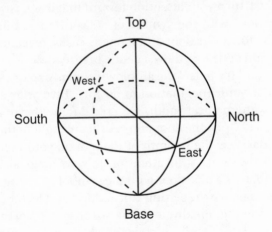

Figure 3. *The magic sphere.*

THE INNER TEMPLE

Having opened the temple using the magic rings, you can now make use of a little-known technique that involves the use of an inner temple. This is an imaginary temple that exists in your mind, yet is an extremely valuable and powerful magical aid. Let your attention be fixed on the uppermost point of the magic sphere and imagine that you see a crown. This can be as ornate or as simple as you like. Let your imagination be your guide as to how this looks. It is your own ideas that matter, and not something copied from someone else. This point represents the out-flowing power of infinite intelligence and life force otherwise known as God. It should be regarded as a positive Father-force and may be visualized as abundant and beneficial energy pouring down into the temple. At the base of the sphere, imagine another symbol—a cube of solid rock that, in turn, symbolizes the Earth-Mother. Imagine fertile Earth with the abundance of growth found in Mother Nature, and try to feel the enormous energy of the earth rising up to assist you.

Next, turn your attention toward magical East. See a yellow door with the symbol of a sword on it. Imagine that you touch the door and it opens easily, revealing the rising Sun at dawn. Allow a gentle breeze to flow into the temple and try to feel the air blowing gently against your skin. Use your imagination to do this. Turn your attention toward magical South. See a red door with a magical wand on it. Open the door and see the full light of the Sun at midday. Feel the warmth of the Sun on your face and body. Now, direct your attention toward magical West, where there is a blue door with the symbol of a chalice on it. Open this, see the setting Sun at dusk, and feel the cool of the evening. Finally, look toward magical North and see a green door with a circular shield on it. Envision the device on the shield (a golden Encircled Cross on a black background will serve you well at this stage). Open the door and see a clear, starlit night sky, while feeling the peace and tranquillity of the night.

This exercise has the effect of increasing your contact with life's energies by supplying additional symbols to the existing scheme. Once again, your subconscious mind will recognize these if they are practiced carefully and patiently. The end result is bound to be one of more effective control. However, in order to get maximum benefit from your magical work, you will need an additional piece of information, one that is quite unique, original, and unknown to most practitioners.

Having established the magic sphere and the four gateways of the elements, you have a basic plan that cannot fail to serve you well if used with purpose. The only thing lacking in this scheme is something to symbolize the center in your imagination. There are many obvious advantages to this, if you care to think about it. One of these is that, as the center *is* the subconscious, anything that symbolizes this is bound to be extremely powerful, provided that you use it correctly.

Having opened the four doorways as described, all you have to do is imagine that you are standing inside a magical temple. The shape, size, and decor are entirely up to you. This is important, because any inner temple must be individual—it must be your own. Spend some time thinking about this and give yourself lots of scope, for temples are many and varied. As a guide, some people like to imagine something similar to a church or cathedral, others prefer a castle, a pyramid, or even a stone circle. Take your time and allow ideas to arise in your mind. Of course, this need not be confined to a ritual—you can do this at any time. The only stipulation is that, whatever the nature of your inner temple, it should have four doorways that equate to the elements and the central symbol of a magical pool of water. Here the symbol of the pool may be surrounded with ornate carvings and designs. Out of the pool pours a constant stream of water, sparkling with brightly colored light. All the colors of the rainbow are contained in this water, in fact every color that ever existed, or will ever exist, can be seen. The pool symbolizes your subconscious mind and the waters are the Waters of Life. It would be fair to say that no two people will have the same ideas or visual images of an inner temple. Each one is different by virtue of the fact that no two people are alike. It is, therefore, not possible for me to give you an exact guide as to what shape or form your temple should take. I can, however, help you find your own way by using this specially constructed exercise as an inner journey. This exercise will help you contact your subconscious mind in a special way, which will then cause your subconscious to give you ideas and images from which you can build this vital state of awareness.

All you have to do is find somewhere quiet, preferably a spare room or, if you are lucky enough, a temple. Relax and clear your mind of everyday thoughts. Then simply perform the following exercise. Do not try to visualize or strain in any way. Simply think of the inner journey, while letting your imagination work for you.

Journey to the Inner Temple

Breathe slowly and gently. Relax, leaving behind all thoughts of everyday life. Let nothing concern you other than the exciting possibilities that lie ahead as you journey to a special place—a place that exists in the deepest recesses of your mind. This is a special place; it is yours; it belongs to no one else. None can enter this place save those few you choose to invite for reasons of your own. In this place, you are in control, you are the master, you direct and you receive. Inside this place, there are natural forces in abundant supply. They are yours to use, yours to understand, for they are part of you. They are the life force and they give form under your direction. Relax and let the vast potential of your subconscious mind work for you, for this is the secret of all magical work. Trust and believe in the power that is you.

Before you, there is a doorway that leads to this special place, your inner temple. It is not difficult to enter, because this is your doorway to your own inner reality. No one can prevent access to this inner realm, and there is nothing to fear, for nothing harmful can ever exist in this inner realm. Walk toward the door in your imagination and, as you do, notice an inscription over the top of the door that says: "When people break the sacred taboos of nature they set into motion the instrument of their own destruction." Now reach out your hand and touch the door. It opens quite easily. When you pass through the door, you find yourself in a large square room. Emblazoned on the floor is the symbol of the Encircled Cross. It seems to be made of pure light and its colors change constantly, in what appears to be a random pattern, yet is not. For the colors change in conformity with the tides of nature.

Now you come to a magical pool of water in the center of this temple. This is the central symbol. This symbol is valid for a variety of reasons that lie outside the scope of this book. Rest assured, however, that this symbol will become a major factor in the success of your magical work. [The use of the pool is fully discussed in chapter 4 and in the practical work on page 57, where this simple idea is put into effective practice.]

Set in each of the four walls is a door. You can pass through any one of these, as you will. The wall immediately in front of you has in it a yellow door with a sword set above it. Touch the door and it opens to reveal a path that leads toward the rising Sun at dawn. You feel a gentle breeze blowing softly against your skin.[1] To your right, there is a red door with a magical wand set above it. Touch this door and it opens to reveal a path that is lit by the midday Sun. Feel the warmth of the summer day. Behind you is a blue door with a chalice set above it. Touch this door and it opens to reveal a path that leads gently down to the sea, lit by the setting Sun. Feel the cool of the evening. Finally, to your left is a green door with a magical shield set above it. Touch this door and it opens to reveal a path lit only by starlight. Feel the peace and tranquillity of the night. All four doors are now open. Now look at the central pool. It is no ordinary pool. The water is not really water, it is power and energy. Later on, you will learn how to use this.

You are now standing in the inner temple. This is an ancient place, to which many have traveled before you and many will follow. For in this place, there are special things to discover. Others have searched and found their own place. Now you must do the same. The task is not difficult. In fact, it is far easier than you think. All you have to do is desire it and you will find this place. I cannot describe it clearly for you, for you are the only person who knows where it is and how it looks. It may be a cave, a secret grove, a temple set on top of a mountain or deep beneath the earth. Seek and you will find it. Now it is time to leave this special place, carrying its memories deep within you. You may return as often as you wish, for this place belongs to you. It has many secrets and contains much in the way of practical knowledge in magical matters. Before you is another door with an Encircled Cross carved deeply into the wood. Touch this door in your imagination, see it open, pass through it, and you are back in your own world once more.

---

[1] When allowing power into your inner temple, you can use geographical imagery, as in the example above, or abstract color, as illustrated on page 26.

It is a good idea to keep notes on these inner-world experiences. No need for long-winded essays, however. Short notes will do. One day, they may prove to be quite valuable, even if they do not appear to make sense at the moment. Often, images from the depths of the subconscious mind appear to be difficult to translate, because you are learning a new language—symbolism. If you persevere, however, you will eventually learn the ways of the subconscious mind. When you are familiar with this inner journey and have found that special place, your own inner temple, you may ritualize this by erecting the triple rings of cosmos as described. Then use your imagination to enter the now-familiar inner temple.

By performing your magical work within this framework, you will notice a distinct improvement in your work, because you are dealing directly with your subconscious mind in a highly personal way. The inner temple will teach you many things, in a way that is difficult to describe, if you have the will and the patience to find it. Having found it, keep it to yourself. Keep it a secret, for this place is not meant to be the subject of general discussion.

Imagining Two Things at Once

How is it possible to see the magic sphere in your mind's eye, while imagining something else, such as opening the magic sphere, or imagining the four gateways and central pool? In other words, how can you imagine two things at once?

It is all a question of memory. To imagine several different things all at the same time would, of course, be difficult, if not impossible. Fortunately, you do not need to do this. As you build up the magic sphere, you establish each part in your memory, moving on through each successive stage and concentrating only on whatever is necessary. For instance, start with the central light, imagining that this exists. Then move on to the next stage, imagining the first of the six arms. There is no need to keep the image of the central light constantly in your imagination, because it is presumed to exist and, in fact, does exist—in your memory. You use this and similar procedures in everyday life. For instance, suppose you are standing in a room facing a window. You see the window quite clearly. If you turn round to face the opposite wall, you, of course, see the wall instead. But you still know that the window exists, because you have just seen it. In fact, you can recall it in your imagination, because its image is stored in your memory. In a similar fashion, having become familiar with the room, you know what the room looks like in totality, without actually seeing it physically.

It is exactly the same with the magic sphere and inner "seeing." In other words, use your imagination to build up an imaginary room in your memory. All through the building process, you establish each stage in your memory before moving on to the next. Therefore, you are free to concentrate on the central pool, knowing that the magic sphere exists in your memory, because you have put it there.

At the end of the ritual, you must inform your subconscious mind that these images are no longer established, hence the need for a closing procedure. Never forget that, although the magic sphere is imaginary and it would be easy to dismiss the entire concept as worthless, it is not. Any *deliberate* erection of a symbolic pattern affects the subconscious mind, because it uses a powerful language that the subconscious mind understands. It is, therefore, necessary to treat these symbols with respect and practice using them often.

CANDLES

By now, the ideas given elsewhere that advocate lighting a candle and speaking some poetic words in the hope that the gods may oblige you, should be seen for what they really are—silly! What you need is common sense and a more scientific approach. Hopefully, this book will go a long way toward giving you a more sensible basis for growth.

You have spent a great deal of time looking at the inner work, using your imagination. This imaginative work is the key to success. Without it there can only be failure and disappointment. However, this is only part of the procedure, albeit an important one. The other half of magical work is concerned with the equipment you use as a focus for your mind. Obviously, in this book, candles are the main focus, so I offer advice on their use.

To begin with, it really doesn't matter what type of wax is used in the making of candles, so do not be fooled into buying expensive and unnecessary beeswax. Paraffin wax is perfectly well suited to candle-magic rituals. With regard to shape, this is a matter of choice. Always choose your candles carefully. Think about them, rather than just purchasing a package of household candles from a hardware store. There are numerous designs available, some specially made for magical work. The more you think about your choice of candle, the better the end result will be—and for a very good reason. By considering this, you are getting involved in your magical work and performing the important function of building up a relationship between you and your intended focus —the candle. So often, this simple routine is missed from magical work. Yet it makes profound sense, from a variety of viewpoints. Become involved with your magic and your equipment and you are bound to be more successful. Think about it in this way: if you acquire something in a matter of fact way, you are unlikely to appreciate it. If you select and choose and consider carefully, the end product is sure to be far more satisfying and rewarding.

Never forget that a candle acts as a focus for your mind. In other words, it is a point of concentration. It is also symbolic. It represents something tangible, such as a desire, a person, or even a type of energy. Unless you (and your subconscious) understand what each candle represents or symbolizes, your ritual will be as pointless as trying to knit fog! In magic, especially candle magic, each candle is a potent magical tool, not, as some would have you believe, because the candle is magical, but because it is special by virtue of choice and symbolism. The lighting of a candle is also symbolic by virtue of the fact that you have activated the intention that is an integral part of that candle. For instance, suppose that you have a candle that represents healing. This, of course, would be chosen with great care, based on the nature of the desire and, perhaps, the type of energy being used. By itself, the candle, therefore, represents an intention that is, at present, quite dormant. When the candle is lit during the ritual, you activate that intention in a rather unique way. You, in fact, say to your subconscious mind: "When I light this candle, may all that it represents come true." As you can now see, there is a world of difference between this approach and the medieval practices advocated by other sources.

Magical and Personal Oils

Magical and personal oils have a number of uses before and during a ritual. Used for personal anointing, different scents have different uses that correspond to individual intentions. The simplest form of anointing is to make a cross or mark on the forehead and the back of the hands. See list of correspondences on page 45.

The following blends are made specifically for anointing. Each can be a blend of pure essential oils, aromatic essences, and appropriate, high-quality, nut-based carrier oils. The power of perfume to invoke magical energy is well known as specific aromas are redolent of psychic states and magical power. Do not use or rub into sensitive skin. The best way of making these is to use approximately 5 parts alcohol to 1 part essential oil. If the mixture is too strong add more alcohol. It works best when matured for a month or two, shaking daily.

The Sun: Frankincense Oil
The Moon: Jasmine Oil
Mercury: Lavender Oil
Venus: Rose Oil
Mars: Benzoin Oil
Jupiter: Sandalwood Oil
Saturn: Musk Oil

Another form of annointing is the charging or consecration of equipment, talismans, seals, or amulets. After the appropriate power has been concentrated into the article, it is sealed with a touch of oil. A talisman is sealed by touching the center, a ritual knife (athame) by having the oil smeared the length of its blade in a single stroke.

Oil is also used to anoint or "dress" candles by various methods. The point of the candle is the wick or "lighting point." The candle is normally held with the point away from you. If you wish to draw something or someone to you, the candle should be anointed from point to base, toward you. If you wish to banish something or someone from your life, the candle is anointed from base to tip, away from you. The third method is used only for healing and is a combination of the first two methods. If you are ill or someone you know is ill, you wish to cure or banish the disease, but you also want to draw good health and healing power to the person or to yourself. This can be done by finding the middle of the candle and using a pin to scratch the patients name around the perimeter. Then anoint the candle from the base to this center line, away from you. Use five drops of oil and five strokes. Still holding the candle, anoint it again from the point to the center line, toward you, using six drops of oil and six strokes. To apply the oil, simply, dip the tip of your finger into the oil and make one stroke, dip again for your second stroke, and so on. You can put all of the strokes in the same place on the candle, or space them around the circumference. What matters most is that, while you are performing the ritual procedure, you must concentrate on what you want. If you are drawing in luck, love, or good health, see it flowing toward you. If you are banishing illness, imagine the misfortune or ill health leaving you.

A seven-knobbed wishing candle is not anointed down its length. Each point is anointed individually. As with all magical work, however, it is the concentration of will that matters.[2] The ritual procedure is designed only to focus your mind's power, or your "desire power," as it is known. You can buy the most expensive equipment available and it will be useless without that desire power. Candles, oils, and incense are the tools that help make your job easier. Many operators add one drop of their own *prima materia* (blood or bodily fluid) to oils and waters to personalize them even further.

Working with Incense

Some people are reluctant to burn traditional incense because they think that an expensive and elaborate incense burner is required. Nothing could be further from the truth. It is very easy to make your own incense burner, using a fireproof metal or earthenware bowl about three inches in diameter. A sugar bowl is ideal, or a chrome ice

---

[2] Seven-knobbed wishing candles have the advantage of being made especially for magical work.

cream sundae dish, or a cat food can, cleaned out and placed on a saucer. There are many other eminently suitable containers as well. Fill your chosen container to within an inch of the rim with clean sand. (You can obtain this from a builder or pet store.) The depth of the sand should not be less than an inch. Stand the bowl on a fireproof surface and you are ready to begin burning your incense.

To use the burner, place a charcoal ring on the sand. Moisten it with methylated spirit, alcohol, or eau de cologne. Then put a match to the charcoal. When the flame has died down and the charcoal is glowing red hot, sprinkle a little incense on it. This method is not only cheap and easy, it is more effective than any incense burner on the market. You can also use self-igniting charcoals, which can be purchased from most metaphysical bookstores.

It should also be noted that this is the best way to obtain the subtlety of fragrance from traditional incense. Modern developments such as "self-igniting" incense are a reluctant concession. This means that the surface is impregnated with saltpetre (potassium nitrate) so that a match touched to the side speedily ignites the block. This, in theory, should work, but the charcoal starts up with a hectic fizz and may splutter out in the middle of a meditation. However, many people have used self-igniting charcoal successfully. It may depend on the brand you buy.

All incense and perfumes are nothing but smelly substances. The magic comes from deep within you. Fragrances are simply aids, focusing tools to narrow down and concentrate your will and mind to accomplish what you wish, when you wish it. If you think that one or more ingredients is out of place, take it out! The incense must work for you or your group. Some of the recipes scattered throughout this book have been put together over centuries by people who have devoted a lot of time to it— sometimes their whole lives! I have also included some recipes of my own.

Element Correspondences

1. The Air element governs dawn, springtime, and intelligence, and is used in all rituals symbolizing new beginnings, healing, travel, learning, writing, recording, communication, illusions, and most magical operations aimed at persuasion.
2. The Fire element governs noon, summertime, and idealism, victory in just conflicts, entertainments, enjoyment, love, gold, riches, and all kinds of luxuries and symbols of power and status.
3. The Water element governs dusk, autumn, and the emotions. It is especially concerned with cleansing, and both invoking and banishing, as well as childbirth, shipping, women's health, discouraging unwelcome guests, growing and harvesting crops, and all forms of Moon magic.
4. The Earth element governs night, winter, all the practical material aspects of life, the home, mining, and minerals, as well as the discovery of hidden treasures and all kinds of monetary gain.

ELEMENT INCENSES

The power of incense and scent lies in its ability to bypass conscious awareness and reach the primordial realms of the mind. It is a dangerously effective instrument in the hands of anyone who wishes to manipulate animal or human behavior. Link any smell you choose with an emotional experience such as love, fear, or joy, and you can recall that emotion at any time by means of the perfume. The smell of a dentist's office will cause stress in most people. To the girl who has fallen in love with her dentist, however, it can be a veritable aphrodisiac. Similarly, a woman who adds a hint of her favorite perfume to a love letter is using magic of the most potent kind, because the recipient will recall the circumstances and emotions of their most torrid encounters.

It would be nice if the place where you work and where you mix and compound the ingredients of your scents was murky and romantic—some deep dungeon or a circular tower, perhaps—but for most of us that is not the case. In fact, the kitchen in an ordinary apartment or house contains more than enough good tools for you to use. You can mix your incense by the light of a fluorescent lamp, if you wish. The cauldron can boil just as well using natural gas or electricity. If you don't have a cauldron, use a nonstick saucepan; a small start is better than none at all. Try some of the recipes given here. Try them first as written, then change them and note the difference. Keep a diary and write about your results. If you can think of a certain music that works well with a certain scent, note that as well.

Some ingredients are becoming difficult to obtain, or are so rare that it is out of the question to use them. Dittany of Crete, for example, is hard to find. It can be replaced in Earth magic by peat moss or oakleaf mold from the forest. A kitchen garden can be pressed into service quite happily. It is simplest to start with the four elemental incenses—Air, Fire, Water, and Earth.

For Air: Balm of Gilead, brown sticky buds that give off an ethereal smoke.

For Fire: Frankincense, a gum resin that comes from the tall tree, *boswellia thurifera,* in the Himalayas. Frankincense is the best incense in the world. It represents the Sun, solar fires, and warmth (more on the planetary recipes later).

For Water: Myrrh, a dark bitter resin collected from the tall scrubby *commiphora myrrha*. It grows along the coast of the Red Sea.

For Earth: Dittany of Crete, as I mentioned earlier, is now very rare. Substitute peat moss or oakleaf mold.

The following recipes have been created for the four elements. Planetary recipes appear later, in chapter 5.

Air Incense
4 parts balm of Gilead
½ part mastic
½ part amber resin grains

Water Incense
4 parts gum myrrh
1 part cut white willow
A dash of sage oil
A dash of menthol crystals
A pinch of mint

Fire Incense
6 parts frankincense
1 part dragons' blood powdered resin
1 part oil of cloves
A small amount of oil of cinnamon

Earth Incense
4 parts peat moss (by volume)
1 part patchouli oil
1 part balsam of Peru
1 part frankincense
1½ ground rosemary leaves (if the mixture is too sticky add more peat moss and more powdered rosemary)

WORKING WITH
ONE ELEMENT AT A TIME

Here is a useful paradigm to illustrate how to work with only one element. Before you start this ritual you should have a definite aim in mind. If you play games with your subconscious mind, it may never take you seriously, so always remember that magic must have some purpose, even if it is only learning or discovering. This ritual will help you acquire power. It will also educate your subconscious mind to the fact that you are going to use that power. To do this requires only a slight variation in working—but a very important variation, as you will see.

Let us begin at the beginning, with a hypothetical situation. A friend who has recently undergone a serious operation has recovered medically, but cannot seem to get back to his or her normal happy self and life is becoming a misery. This is not normal, as your friend is usually quite a happy person and full of life. You decide to try and help, through magic. Look at the situation in a detached way, then decide if a magical operation can help. If this, indeed, seems to be the answer, which element should you use? Since the problem is an emotional one, you use the Water element.

Now you can plan out the rite. Since you are working with the Water element, you work toward the West, in your imagination, during the conjuration of power. You use a blue altar cloth and place a bowl of water at the West to signify that this quarter is being worked. Before performing the rite, it is a good idea to have a rehearsal, so that any problems can be spotted and put right. After your pre-rite relaxation, you set aside a period of contemplation on the desired result, so that you can clear your mind and assure yourself that the rite is going to work. It is no good hoping and wishing. You have to *know* that your magic will work.

When you are ready, open the temple as normal, acquiring the "inner weapons," and facing the western quarter.[3] Declare the intention of the rite. This may be written out and read, if you like. In fact, writing a script is always a good idea, as it helps you get more involved in the ritual. Now turn your attention to the central pool. Look at the pool and know that you are about to use its power. If necessary, declare this in some positive way, such as: "I now call on my never-ending supply of subconscious power." See the placid surface change into a huge fountain reaching high into the sky and gleaming with light and power. Now is the time to focus this through the Water element, perhaps using words such as: "I now call upon the Water element to respond to my will and to the true desires of _____ [name the person concerned]." See the fountain change to a brilliant blue, then focus your attention on the chalice that is now gleaming with power. Pass this to your friend, who takes the power contained in it and then returns it to you. Your friend leaves, feeling much better. Sit for a while and contemplate the success of this rite, then see the fountain change to a calm pool again. Close in the usual way leaving the temple and writing up any notes.

These inner visualizations are, of course, only a suggestion. The image of the fountain should remain, but you can change any of the other symbols in any meaningful way you feel is right. For instance, the water of the fountain can rush down the path and out through the doorway to your friend. You can take the water from the fountain in the chalice and give it to your friend to drink, or perhaps your friend can be taken to the fountain to drink or bathe.

---

[3] In candle magic, there is no need for physical weapons. You can work with the inner counterparts, for example, weapons in the imagination. Acquisition is done when the weapon is seen in the imagination emblazoned on the door or inside the elemental door.

This, of course, is all performed as a seated meditation. If you have representations of the physical weapons, you can direct the power into the water contained in the physical magic chalice and drink this yourself, while seeing your friend receive the power. There are many possible permutations; you must decide. With other rites involving one of the other elements, you, of course will change the symbolism to suit the circumstances.

The use of the physical weapons is a good idea, as this helps your mind focus on the physical side of things. This may be taken one stage further by the use of a physical focus for the conjured power. This is known as a talisman.

MAKING AND CHARGING A SIMPLE TALISMAN

It is traditional to draw a talisman on parchment. Nowadays, however, this is not necessary, and any good-quality paper will do. Parchment became popular simply because, in the past, it was the only thing available. Paper had not yet been invented. Do not try to use someone else's designs. These were personal to the people who drew them. Design your own talisman. A talisman must contain three pieces of visual imagery:

A symbol of the power being conjured;
A symbol of the end result required;
Some way of identifying it with the recipient.

In the previous rite, a good talisman might be an Encircled Cross, about two inches in diameter drawn on good-quality paper and marked at the cardinal points, with some special emphasis on the West (perhaps an arrow pointing toward it). Draw this in blue ink, against a background of a cup shining with light, perhaps with the words "happiness restored" written about it. Use your imagination. On the reverse side, write the person's name. Now you have a personal, usable talisman. To use it in the rite requires only a slight change in procedure. At the pool, when the Water element is conjured, imagine the power pouring into the talisman. You can place the talisman in a physical chalice, or on the Ace of Cups card, or wherever you decide. At the end of the rite, put it in a safe place until the desired result is achieved, or, if the recipient is a believer, give it to him or her.

Deactivating talismans is quite simple. Merely reverse the ritual process then destroy it. To save time, you can bury it in the earth, while envisioning the power returning to its source. Look to your imagination for ideas.

The rite may be improved by working into it some means of symbolically neutralizing any blocks to power that may exist. The pool represents the subconscious mind being contacted and used in one of two ways. The weapons symbolize taking conscious control of power. The four doorways are symbolic of the way in which you use power. It is this latter imagery of which you can now make use, when the power has been conjured, either in the imagination or into a talisman. If you are using a talisman, visualize the power pouring out through the doorways to the outside world in a positive way.

Using the previous rite as an example, conjure the Water element. See the cup fill with power, then see this power flow out in four directions into the doorways, one at a time. Since the doorways represent the way in which you express power, you can now choose to express it in a positive way. The Air doorway is the way in which you express yourself through thought; the Fire doorway is the way you express yourself through action; the Water doorway is your means of emotional expression; the Earth doorway is the way you express yourself through the knowledge of past experience. As the power enters the

Air doorway you must make sure it will be expressed properly and not hindered by destructive thinking at some future date. This is done by using positive symbolism. When the power is in the doorway, see it pass through a door with an Encircled Cross emblazoned on it. This symbol represents perfection in the physical sense. You are thus telling your subconscious mind that it is not to be sidetracked in the doorway by unproductive thinking. Do the same with each of the other doorways. Then, see your friend in the center of an Encircled Cross, with the same four doors at the appropriate cardinal points. The power can now be seen to enter the circle through the doorways to your friend. If you are using a talisman, conjure the power through the chalice, then see power flowing out of the talisman in four directions, to the doorways described.

Practice and deep thinking will be needed in order to build this idea into your mind so that any power that passes through it will not meet with unforeseen blocks.

Working with the Four Elements

Here is a spell from the Middle Ages that I have modified to illustrate how medieval paradigms can be used, if you understand what you are doing. This ritual can be performed at any time; however, traditionally, it should be performed on a Friday evening at 9 P.M. for seven consecutive weeks. This is the day and hour of Venus, the Goddess of Love.

A Potent Spell to Secure Love
Using the Four Elements
It is important to utilize the appropriate correspondences —in this case those of the four elements. Use four candles, one for each element (green for Earth, yellow for Air,

red for Fire, and blue for Water.) You will also need a Self
Candle. You will need an altar cloth, incense for each element divided into four equal parts, and the four 10s of
the tarot, if you happen to have a deck available. Having
attended to these preliminaries, all that remains is to
open the temple in the manner already given.

Erect the magic sphere and enter the inner temple. Direct
your attention to the crown. This is, as you know by now,
the symbolic point from which all power flows. It also
equates to the All-Father. Imagine that the crown begins
to glow with a bright light that moves downward into the
inner temple. This power must be allowed into the temple through the four elemental gateways. The four elements are simply four ways in which this power can be
expressed. There are many symbolic ways of expressing
power. This is simply a means of breaking down the over-
all energy pattern into manageable units, rather as a
prism can be split up into different colors. The elemental
doorways are merely a symbolic way of splitting up the
power into manageable units.

With a pencil and paper, draw two entwined hearts
and write inside these your name and the name of the
person you desire to love you. Fold up the piece of paper
and place it under the Self Candle holder on your altar. As
soon as possible after the final ritual, this written wish
should be destroyed symbolically. You can do this in any
way you think suitable: tear it into small pieces and scat-
ter it to the wind, cast it into a lake or stream, bury it in
the ground, or burn it.

Imagine the northern door and light the green candle, saying: "I call the earth to bind my spell." See that
gateway open and try to cultivate a feeling of allowing
power to come in through that gateway. Imagine the
power as under your control. For instance, when you are
dealing with North, see that gateway open and the green
light-power of earth pour in. Feel it coming in as a power.

Do the same with yellow at the East, saying: "Air speed is travel well." Do the same with red for the South, saying: "Fire, give it spirit from above." Finally, facing West in the inner temple in your imagination, say: "May water quench my spell with love."

The four gateways, which equate to the four elements, are the way in which power symbolically enters the inner temple. There are points in this ritual at which each quarter is addressed and each doorway opened using the appropriate word-spell. Power is thereby allowed into the temple and finally impinges on the center. Here, in the center, you are dealing with the magical pool. All this energy builds up in this central pool. In your imagination, change that pool into a fountain of light, a fountain of water, shimmering with light and with power. Use the idea of a fountain, so the power comes in. It comes in through the four elemental gateways, into the center. It erupts there as a fountain of pure power. Now spend a few minutes creatively thinking your picture-symbol of you and your special person into the fountain. That power then goes out through those four gateways into the outside world, carrying your intention with it. Of course, at the conclusion, reverse the procedure and close down the inner temple and magic sphere as previously illustrated.

THE INTENTION CANDLE

Read through this chapter many times, thinking about the ideas given. Practice the techniques of the magic sphere and the inner temple, until you are fully conversant with them. The whole idea is that they should become second nature to you. Nothing can be worse than finding yourself halfway through a ritual wondering what happens next. Get to know your technique to such a degree that this can never happen. A good ritual should flow easily. This can only be achieved when you know what you are doing.

When you are completely satisfied that you are familiar with these techniques, try this very useful ritual exercise. It can prepare the way for many types of candle-burning rites.

RITUAL FOR FOCUSING INTENTIONS

For this, you will need the candles previously mentioned, as well as an additional candle to symbolize a specific intention. This candle may be any color that relates to one of the four elements or your Self Candle. (The planetary forces will be discussed later in this book.)

Follow the guidance given on ritual procedure in chapter 2, starting with the intention of the ritual. This may be anything that you wish. It is entirely up to you. However, do make certain that you are positive about your intention and that you remove all negative thoughts, as suggested previously. Having done this, proceed with the ritual, using the magic sphere and the inner temple. The intention candle, which should be placed in front of the Self Candle, may now be lit. When this is done, focus your attention on the pool.

See this turn into a fountain of water that glows with bright light. Allow this to build up in your imagination for a while, then see this light go out in four directions, through the elemental doorways, carrying your intention with it. If you like, you may sit down for a while and continue to see this happening, all the time being positive, feeling and knowing that your subconscious mind is using energy to achieve its goal.

At conclusion, see the fountain gradually disappear, until you are left with a pool of still water once more. Extinguish the intention candle (this may be left to burn down, if you prefer) and close the rite as usual. Do not forget to back up the ritual by using creative thinking whenever possible, as this helps to keep the channels of power open.

4

THE COSMIC TIDES

Who knows when people first became aware of the idea of time. Long before clocks were invented, how did we track time? Quite simply, people became aware of time by becoming aware of natural phenomena, by observing and using their senses in a different way. When people first noticed that all was not as it seemed, they set foot on the path to reality. Often, especially today, we accept without thinking, without questioning and without really seeing. To become successful at candle magic, however, we must always look, observe, and question.

THE BIRTH OF ASTROLOGY

Just imagine, a few thousand years ago, someone sitting on a rock watching the Sunrise: first, a glimmer of light that gets progressively brighter, and then the welcome glow of the Sun itself as it starts to appear over the horizon. To everyone else, this may not seem particularly important—after all, it happens every day, and there is work to be done. To the rest, the mundane is everything and it will stay that way forever. Nothing will ever change and life is a foregone conclusion. But something is stirring in the mind of this one lone observer. That something is, as yet, unknown, but curiosity is leading into new realms. The others do not understand. They make fun of this morning vigil, as, day by day, our lonely observer watches the Sun rise before yielding to the demands of existence. Over a period of time, this curious soul notices that, when the Sun rises, nature comes alive—animals stir and birds sing. When the Sun is overhead, it is much warmer than at either dawn or dusk. And, as the Sun sets, life slows its pace, in preparation for the nightly sleep. From this correlation of the movement of the Sun to events here on Earth, a primitive kind of astrology was born. Gradually, people learned more and more about solar activity, and then attention was drawn to the Moon, whose shape, they observed, changed in a regular pattern. Further observation revealed that the tides of the sea changed with the phase of the Moon. And, most significantly, they realized that these could be predicted.

From the vantage point of the 20th century we now know that the magnetic pull of the Moon does, indeed, influence the tides. When the Sun and the Moon are in approximately the same position in the sky, there is a New Moon. This generates a high tide through the forces these two bodies exert on each other. At the Full Moon, there is a much lower tide, because the forces of these two bodies tend to compensate for each other. Today, these are accepted astronomical facts, but to ancient thinkers, these forces were something else—they were *gods*. Because they could not understand these phenomena, ancient people personified them. They presumed that some great power, some mighty being, moved through the skies. To identify with this power, they personalized it. They made it into a god—quite a natural thing to do, if you think about it. They recognized something greater than themselves, so they made it superhuman in order to communicate with it—in order to seek its favor and so be granted some of its power. When the Sun God rises, life begins. He casts his light and warmth, and Earth comes to life. When the Sun God is low in the sky, in winter, death is evident and there is coldness and snow. The Moon became the lunar goddess. When she was with the Sun God, the tides were high and the plants grew more quickly. When she was opposed to the Sun God, there was low tide and slower growth.

The more ancient people observed and tried to contact the gods through prayer and sacrifice, the more they learned. The Sun and Moon became more than just lights in the sky. They became benefactors. The images grew and the gods became more personal. Some, who rose above the level of other mortals, became servants of these gods. Their priestly role was to demonstrate the power of the gods. Through their guidance, crops grew better, due to more accurate planting times. Through their prediction of the tides, people fished more productively. And through their ability to predict eclipses, people learned to fear and obey the gods. There was nothing more awesome than the sight of the forces of darkness swallowing up the light of the Sun and plunging the world into darkness. This was enough to raise the worst fears in anybody.

Since those early days, the study of the movement of the planets has become astronomy. The real science, however, is astrology. Unfortunately, there are many misconceptions about astrology. I will attempt to clear these away, so that you may see the value of this magical science.

It is not important that every aspiring candle-magic practitioner should become an astrologer. This is best left to those who wish to study the science in its own right. Just as a housewife need not synthesize various organic chemicals in order to make a cleaning product, a worker of candle magic need not understand all the finer points of astrology. In magic, there are many branches of specialized research—astrology is just one. You can either learn all about it, or you can ask an astrologer for guidance. It is up to you. However, it is always a good idea to have some knowledge of the subject. If you do not know about the planets, how can you use their energies?

Astrology is the study of planetary movements and the relating of such movements to natural events, particularly in human life. The movement of the Sun and Moon relate to natural events on Earth. The error arises when you assume that those heavenly bodies actually cause those events. You should know that the planets do not rule or have influence over anything. To think otherwise is incorrect. You may ask: "What about the Moon and its effects on the tides and plant growth?" In fact, that is simply a matter of magnetic force, and even this is debatable.

COSMIC ENERGY

Magical practitioners must look at the whole subject of astrology and magic in the light of common sense and sound reasoning. For a start, there is energy. This energy is in a state of flux—in other words, it changes constantly, every second of every day. Nothing ever stays the same and nothing will ever be the same again. If you have a way to measure these changes, you can then predict when they will occur and how often. On an obvious level, this is done in astronomy. The position of a planet can be stated years in advance. Eclipses can be timed to the second. Even the exact date of a comet can be given in advance. How is this done? Simply by observation and measurement. Everything in creation works to precise laws, and if you know the laws, you can predict.

When dealing with cosmic energy you do, however, have a problem. First, you cannot see it, measure it, or weigh it. So where do you go, what do you do? Ancient people had the right idea. They used natural events and phenomena as a way of charting and understanding patterns of energy. This is not as difficult as you may think. It is probably best left to serious students of such matters, but the reasoning behind it you will find valuable in your magical work. In order to measure natural energy and equate this to human existence (and, to some extent, predict future possibilities), ancient observers developed a symbolic system of measurement called astrology. They split the heavens into twelve equal portions of thirty degrees each. The whole scheme was named the "zodiac," and the twelve divisions became the now-familiar "signs of the zodiac," Aries, Taurus, Gemini, and so on. By studying the positions of the planets in these signs and observing natural events, they constructed a system of correlations and correspondences. This became astrology. They noticed that each planet related to a specific type of energy and that the sign that contained the planet had a nature all its own. For instance, the planet Mars represented action, energy, and initiative. Its effect depended very much on the sign in which the planet resided. In other words, the sign modified the planetary energy.

If you think about this scheme, you see that it encompasses quite a variety of possibilities. Not only is the planetary placement important, but the angles between the planets also modify the effects. Two planets in the same position are said to be conjunct. This is considered to be a powerful placement, because both are pulling in the same direction, rather like the Sun and Moon at New Moon. Planets in opposition—in other words, 180 degrees apart—are not considered beneficial, because they are pulling in opposite directions, or working against each other. There are, of course, many other possible angles, some considered good, some difficult. These are known as the planetary aspects.

Basic Astrology

Astrology became the most accurate system known for forecasting and measuring the effects of natural energy on human life. It is doubtful that there will ever be another system to surpass it. It suffered from the suppression caused by the Vatican and went underground. Today's astrology is very different than it once was, for some people now think that the Sun sign columns in the newspapers are what astrology is all about. On the other hand, there are professional organizations that research astrological data and who use astrology the way it was once used years ago. However, few people know about it. You should remember that astrology is a *magical* science. Magic and astrology go hand in hand. Magic can work with or without astrology, but astrology without magical knowledge is virtually worthless. Today, you may find some people who masquerade as astrologers who know little of astrology. You may also meet astrologers who know little of magical techniques. It's unfortunate that study of esoteric subjects has become so separated and fragmented. Magic is a great science and astrology is merely part of that science.

Let us look at some of the cosmic tides and see how astrology can help you measure, understand, and even forecast them. When the Sun moves into the sign of Aries, the season of spring begins. The Sun in Cancer heralds summer, in Libra, autumn, and in Capricorn, winter in our latitude. This is indisputable. Every year, without fail, the same seasons will occur in the same order. You can measure the length and predict the arrival of each season without error.

Science argues that it is the angle of Earth that is responsible for these yearly climatic changes—the revolution of Earth around the Sun, they say, is what causes the seasons. Once again, science overlooks the obvious and goes astray. If, indeed, the angle of Earth were responsible, then surely the changes in the seasons would be gradual. Simple observation shows that this is not so. The angle of Earth will, of course, help to alter the temperature and climatic conditions, but can science tell us why seeds start to grow, or buds form on trees in the spring? I have known this to happen, despite a wide variety of temperatures, at approximately the same time each year. It makes no difference whether you have six feet of snow and icy winds, or a warm period. Within a week or so of the Sun entering the sign of Aries, spring comes in and nature comes to life. Do you think that the leaves fall from the trees in autumn? They do, but not at the beginning of autumn. When the Sun enters the sign of Scorpio, the leaves fall, regardless of climatic conditions. It is almost as though there were some cosmic clock that activates these things.

THE COSMIC CLOCK

If you are at all sensitive, you will notice the changes in these solar tides, especially if you are in a temple. Spring and summer are especially noticeable, as the temple is filled with energy. I think you can forget, in this setting, about scientific explanations such as the angle of the Earth and look instead at the magical explanation. On the face of it, it would seem that the position of the Sun in the zodiac is the cause of these changes in energy patterns, resulting, of course, in the change of seasons. If you accept this easy answer, however, you will, like science, be very wrong. Such thinking assumes that the planets exert some influence. They do not. More correctly, there is energy; this energy is constantly changing, according to precise laws; the planets help us understand how this energy applies to life on Earth and assists us in predicting changes in the energy patterns.

It is vitally important that you not assume that the planets cause energy to flow or that these affect life in any way. They are merely pointers or signifiers. A fair analogy might be a clock. By looking at a clock, you know what time it is. You can plan your day by it or take whatever action is appropriate, based on the information it gives you. The clock indicates time, it measures time, but it is not responsible for time. Time exists whether you have a clock or not. The clock merely gives you an indication, a measurement.

Take another example—a traffic light. A traffic light controls the flow of traffic and indicates how the traffic moves. It does not create the traffic in the first place. In this example, the traffic is equivalent to the flow of energy and the traffic light, which indicates the status of traffic flow, is equivalent to a planet. Astrology is like a huge cosmic clock. You can look at it and deduce when things are likely to happen. In the case of the Sun, its position in the zodiac tells you when the seasons of the year will occur. But what about the other planets? Can these be used to tell the time in the same way? Yes they can. However, this clock is far more complex than the one you buy in a shop and is, consequently, far more useful.

In addition to the position of a planet, the nature of the planet also serves to help identify the nature of the cosmic energy flow. The nature of the Sun, for instance, is vitality, power and life. Its position in the zodiac will tell you how this power is being applied and how life on Earth will be affected. Similarly, the nature of Saturn is limitation and restriction. Its zodiac position will indicate how this restriction is applying to Earth. So the planetary positions and the angles between these planets are an indication of the flow of natural energy. But what of this energy? Does this mean you are subjected to this flow whether you like it or not? Is your life a foregone conclusion? In other words, from the moment of birth, is your life already mapped out? It is important that you ask these questions. It is also important that you look a little deeper for the truth.

On the face of it, it seems that fate or destiny, call it what you will, indeed rules your life. There are two patterns of life on this planet, that of nature and that of humanity. Nature responds fully to the cosmic clock—it is predictable. Human beings, however, have one important difference in their nature—choice. Please disregard the rambling's of fools who talk about fate and predestination. There is, in truth, no such thing. If you are conditioned to accept these silly ideas, your fate is indeed predestined. Just as the tides respond in predictable ways, so will you. You can, at any time, take your life into your own hands and determine your own future. You have the choice. Sometimes, this may appear impossible, but it is nevertheless true. Centuries of superstition and unrealistic thinking have given you ideas of fate, karma, and other such restrictive dogmas. Just because some popular prophet declared what he or she thought was the truth doesn't mean that he or she is correct, or that you have to accept those beliefs. Many prophets were little better than arrogant fools—the blind leading those even more blind. Nor does this apply only to the past. It is just as true today.

The real position of humanity in relation to cosmic energy and life is this: there is abundant energy. You use this energy according to your needs and you have total free choice in the way in which you use it. There are no limits, no restrictions, and no laws that tell you what you must and must not do—none that have not been invented by ourselves. You are far greater and infinitely more powerful than you realize. Religion and the teachings of the truly blind may have limited your awareness of this truth and have given you false patterns of belief—such as sin, retribution, eternal damnation, and other such stupidity. Because of these ideas, you have, to a large extent, become predictable, but this need not be so. You always have a choice. Exercise that choice and the might of cosmic energy will rush to your aid. Naturally, free choice will not put money into the coffers of organized religions or cult movements and it will not help the inflation of some master's ego—little wonder that they do not want you to think for yourself.

Your birth chart is a map of your potential. You do not have to be an astrologer to realize this potential. You only have to decide what you want and then have the courage to exercise free choice, using cosmic energy to fulfill your desires. Follow the guidelines this book gives you and you will do just that.

The study of astrology, human potential, and even energy itself is very rewarding. Unless you feel the need to study such things in detail, however, you should not. In all things, be natural. The world teaches that you become qualified in something in order to get anywhere. This leads you to be motivated by so-called intellectual pursuits. In magic, you have no such restrictions. Intellectual searching is left to the individual. Your pattern of study and learning is entirely your own affair. You do not have to pass an examination to become a true witch or magician. Success is measured by results. It does not matter if you cannot tell the difference between the planet Jupiter and the Morning Star. All that matters is your ability to be yourself and to have whatever you wish. If you feel the need to study various magical arts, such as astrology, then do so. It is not compulsory. In magic and in life itself, nothing is compulsory. Laziness, on the other hand, or the attitude of wanting everything for little effort, is inexcusable. Little effort begets little results. Dedication and persistence are the way to success.

Apart from being a blueprint for success, your birth chart will reveal much more, especially to those skilled in astrology.[1] Your own planetary positions at birth indicate

---

[1] A birth chart may be obtained in the United States from Llewellyn's Personal Astrological Services, as advertized in *New Worlds of Mind and Spirit* magazine. Contact Personal Services, c/o Llewellyn, P.O. Box 64383, St. Paul, MN 55164. In England, birth charts are available from *Prediction* magazine. Write to Readers' Services, c/o Prediction, Link House, Dingwall Avenue, Croydon, Surrey CR9 2TA, England.

your potential. The planetary movements since that date indicate how energy will apply itself to your Earth life. By comparing these two, you gain an accurate picture of how these energies are likely to affect you and your potential for years to come. It is possible to predict with a fair degree of accuracy how your life will be affected. More importantly you can now know in advance which energies are affecting you and where. And, even more important, you can know how you can use these energies.

A QUESTION OF TIME

It is important to select, not only the correct time, but also the correct time for a particular act of magic. Consider the following factors:

> Should the act take place in the hours of daylight or darkness?
> Is the day of the week of any importance?
> Is the date of any importance?
> Is the phase of the Moon as critical as some authorities have indicated?
> Is it necessary to take the astrological situation into account?

There are several ways of classifying the hours of the day and the days of the week under planetary headings. These range from the classical and apparently arbitrary "doctrine of signatures" to the more modern, but still arbitrary, system that uses atomic clocks in conjunction with the older method of attributing all things to planetary categories.

Many attempts have been made to relate natural tides to magical work. So far, none of these have been successful, due to lack of thought and a good measure of superstition. One such attempt relies on planetary hours and the days of the week. The idea that a planet rules anything should, by now, be consigned to the dustbin, where it rightly belongs. The idea that a planet rules certain days of the week is just as absurd, so please forget it. To presume that you can only work lunar magic on the day of the Moon (in other words, on Monday) is self-restricting. Who is really ready to say that the Moon (or, to be more correct, lunar energy) ceases to exist for the other six days? Yet some astrologers and magicians accept this concept without a second thought. What a pity! If you cannot do it on a Monday, then you simply cannot do it! Absurd! Yet you will find this sort of absurdity taught in the "secret arts." Please forget about planetary days.

Planetary hours are just as ridiculous. It was thought that certain hours were ruled by certain planets. This provided a convenient "system" for working with astrology and horary charts, or mundane charts. The idea that you can divide the day and night into equal sections and then allot a planet to each of these sections, or hours, is senseless as far as I'm concerned. This system, if it can be called a system, is out of date because, like the previous concept of planetary days, it bears no resemblance to what is actually going on in the heavens.

You do not need to concern yourself with planetary hours and days, these are used for specific techniques by advanced students of astrology and not by beginners. The old system of planetary hours is, I assure you, not based on fact. Dividing the day and night into 12 equal portions may well work at the equator but not at northern or southern latitudes. A true planetary hour may vary from as little as 50 minutes to as much as 3 hours. The times of these planetary hours vary according to location. It is also sheer nonsense to base planetary rulerships on the days of the week—this is pure superstition rather than fact. For instance, the first hour of Saturday is supposed to be ruled by Saturn. Taking any Saturday in July, using corrected planetary hours charts, where I am writing from at this point in time (British Isles) you would find that the Moon is in fact applying. If you really wish to be this precise, you can have these charts calculated for you and your present location. All you need to do is track down one of the many fine astrologers who know the science well enough. These charts can be of great value in everyday life such as using the Mercury hour for writing important letters, or the Jupiter hour for creating opportunities.

I think that the best system of charting cosmic energy is by using astrology and your natal chart. Astrology is, after all, the science of energy patterns. You start with your personal plan of potential, your birth chart, and deduce from this which planets rule the main areas of your life. Since your birth, the planets have continued to carry on, moving around the heavens, constantly indicating how energies are applying to Earth life. They also show how the energies have been applying to you as an individual. When the planets move around your birth planets they are called "transiting" planets. When any one of these planets forms a certain angle or aspect to the position of one of the planets in your chart (known as a natal planet), something rather special happens. Energy flows. And this energy can be used.

There are three kinds of aspects—good, difficult, and neutral. A "good" aspect means that the transiting planet is affecting your natal planet in a useful and beneficial way, thereby enhancing the area of life ruled by the natal planet. In case you find this confusing, I will give you an example. Suppose the planet Venus rules money in your birth chart. A good aspect from a transiting planet could help produce more money in your life. You have a choice. The potential is there to increase money supply. If you take it, you are working with the natural tides, so success is that much easier. Naturally, much depends on the nature of the transiting planet. For instance, a Jupiter transit could bring in the opportunity to make more money. A Saturn transit can help you save more money and consolidate. The important thing to know is what the natal planet rules, the nature of the aspect, and the nature of the transiting planet. Put all this together and you have a fair picture of how events are likely to move in your life.

Now, of course, you come to the opposite side of the coin—the difficult aspect. This may mean trouble, torment, problems, or worries. A difficult aspect implies problems, but these are not insurmountable. Remember, there is no compulsion in the cosmic scheme of energy. If you do not do anything about a difficult aspect, things may well get out of hand, largely due to the ideas with which society has conditioned you. If, however, you choose to deal with that difficult aspect, you may succeed, not only in removing the problems, but in turning the aspect to your advantage. The opportunity to better yourself is offered by a so-called difficult aspect. There may well be difficulties, but you can overcome them. The energy to do this is there, waiting to be used.

For example, assume that Venus rules money in your birth chart, but this time, with a difficult aspect from Jupiter. The general tendency may be to squander and overspend, and gains may easily be lost. This inclination, if unchecked, tends toward the negative side of Jupiter— in other words, toward overexpansion. The first step, in this case, is to recognize what is causing the problem. Then you must do something about it, using magical techniques.

The third aspect possibility is when no transits occur. This is called the neutral aspect. Generally speaking, this means that the status quo will remain. There is no inclination to do anything, either positive or negative. Remember, however, that you can still work effective rituals. You will probably need to concentrate more, but you can, if necessary, still use the energy of the unaspected natal planet. I should, in all fairness, state that you do not have to plan your rituals according to these tides of energies. A pure, sustained thought or desire, backed up by persistent magical work, will eventually get results. The important thing to remember when using this system is that you need to get to know what the planets mean for you. In other words you need to know which areas of life are ruled by each planet.[2] You also need to know the nature of each planet, as this will enable you to judge the type and effect of the transit. As for the rest, there is no need to spend years learning astrology, unless, as I have said, you wish to do so. There are numerous cosmic tides, and therefore, many types of charts. New ones are being discovered all the time. Most of these, however, are of a specialized nature and need not concern you here and now.

DISCOVERING YOUR PERSONAL CONTACT WITH POWER

Experiment in your own way, carefully recording lunar and planetary aspects and positions and thereby coming to conclusions that are as personal as the way your own methods of working magic will evolve. Alternatively, you can organize a routine of lunar observations, recording your emotional impressions and clarity of imagination. Thereafter, perform magic only during phases or aspects when you feel most powerful and your imagination is most vivid.

---

[2] This paradigm is fully discussed in my book, *The Magickian: A Study in Effective Magick*. York Beach, ME: Samuel Weiser, 1993.

5

THE POWER OF PLANETS

Magic is the science of using and understanding your subconscious mind—your personal "God within." All else is subservient to this essential truth. Candles, robes, incense, chants, and conjurations are simply tools that, in the right hands, can successfully encourage the cooperation of the unlimited power of your subconscious mind. How is this possible? What is the subconscious? After all, you cannot see it or touch it.

Despite the views of science, which insist that all must be measurable, you do not have to see or touch something to prove it exists. Can any scientist actually help you "see" electricity, or present you with a half pound of it? No, of course not—yet it does exist. You cannot see, or even smell, oxygen, yet you know it exists in the atmosphere and that, without it, you would die. The proof lies, not in measurement, but in use. You use electricity, you use (breathe) oxygen, and you use the power of the subconscious mind, usually without knowing it. What regulates your breathing or heartbeat? What heals your wounds or caused your body to grow when you were young? The answer is your subconscious mind, or, to be more specific, part of this mind. Think about the countless "automatic" functions within your body. All of these are controlled on your behalf, without difficulty or any effort on your part. Can you imagine how difficult, even impossible, life would be if you had to think about these things and organize them yourself?

Your subconscious mind is sufficiently powerful to handle anything you ask of it, in addition to carrying out all these functions it has controlled since your birth. Little wonder that the subconscious is often known as an inner god or temple of the mind. For centuries, knowledgeable people have tried to tell humanity that they are the masters of their own destinies, that they really do have power and that the god within is the key to all things. Regrettably, few ever listen, preferring instead to accept the self-limiting dogmas of religion, the superstitious practices of modern esoterics, or the rambling of a spirit guide. If you wish for success, happiness, and power, seek the god within. You do not need a priest or a guru to do this, or any other intermediary. All you need is the determination to find that which is already yours—the limitless power of your own subconscious mind.

As this is a book of practical magic, it will confine itself to the ability of the subconscious mind to affect physical matter. How is this possible? Simply because everything on Earth, or indeed in the whole of the universe, is made up of inert matter enlivened by energy or life force. Energy is everywhere. Nothing could exist without it. Change the type of energy and you change the appearance and nature of the inert matter that contains it. For instance, a pear and a cabbage appear to have little in common in terms of shape, taste, or growth pattern. Yet, from a cosmic point of view, the essential difference lies simply in the type of energy each contains. Do not dismiss this as fantasy—it is not. The alchemists of old sought the secret of transmutation, or the ability to change base metals into gold. There are stories that some succeeded! Modern science can now change the nature of matter by using nuclear bombardment to alter the atomic structure of certain materials. By doing this, they are simply altering the energy pattern, thereby proving the theories that sensible modern practitioners of magic have been expounding for some considerable time.

If you can accept the paradigm that matter can be affected by altering the pattern of energy within it, you should, at the same time, throw out the mistaken concept that this can only be done in an atomic pile. Your subconscious mind uses life-energy to achieve results by changing energy patterns to suit your needs. Once again, look at the automatic functions of your own body. When you cut yourself, the wound heals and that ugly cut is transformed into new skin. A physical condition has been changed because your subconscious mind has altered it on your behalf, changing the appearance of the wound using natural energy. If it can perform this minor miracle without any effort on your part, think what it can do if you give it precise instructions!

The ability of your subconscious mind to direct life-energy and thereby change the nature of matter is the crux of realistic magical practices. By affecting matter, you affect circumstances, and thereby, your entire future. There are alternative theories involving gifts from the gods, cosmic beings who look after the world (not very successfully, you should note), and the really addle-brained philosophies of karma. Compare the two points of view. On the one hand, you have the scientific paradigm of subconscious power, while, on the other, you have the doctrines of despair backed up by "escape clauses" that blame intangibles such as God's will or an unprovable karmic debt when things go wrong—as they inevitably do! Now is the time to consider these things and make the more sensible choice of reality, as explained by scientific magic.

An essential part of magical training is an understanding of energy. You must understand energy, so that you can use it more successfully. There can be little doubt that the variety of energy patterns and the complexity of the scheme seems, at first, too vast and daunting to be understood with ease. Fortunately, this is not the case, provided that you use scientific methods to approach the topic. The secret lies in categorizing energies under recognizable headings. For instance, take plants. The word "plants" acts as a main category, excluding all other things on this planet. If you break this category into subheadings, such as "vegetables," "flowers," and "weeds," each of these can then be further divided into varieties and species. The whole object of the exercise is not to create complexity, for that already exists. Rather, it helps us understand the whole subject far more easily. Any plant can now be identified and understood far better due to classification. You apply the same idea to life's energies by using the planets.

THE PLANETS

Right from the start, discard the idea that the planets directly affect life here on Earth. While it can legitimately be proved that the Moon affects the tides, it is wrong to assume that the planet Saturn, for instance, which is several hundred million miles away and barely perceptible to the naked eye, can have any direct effect on Earth life. The mistake probably arose from a lack of understanding of the term "planetary rulership." Any competent astrologer or magical worker knows that the word "rule" does not imply control by a physical body existing in space. What it actually means is that certain physical objects or events *correspond* to the essential nature of an energy that in turn equates to the classical idea of the inner meaning of a planet. For example: the color red, the metal iron, enterprise, initiative, and daring are all "ruled" by the planet Mars. This does not mean that the planet Mars affects these things. It simply means that the energy classified as belonging to Mars is predominant in, or corresponds to, the objects and events mentioned. The word "correspond" should always be borne in mind when dealing with rulership. This will help you to understand the much-misunderstood doctrine of correspondences, or the "doctrine of signatures," as it is sometimes called.

Planetary Correspondences

It is important that you use the correct correspondences in magical work, not because the gods will not be satisfied, but simply because like attracts like. I do not mean that if you put a lump of iron on your altar, it will attract the power of Mars—this is nonsense. I mean that, in the case of Mars energy, the ideas associated with iron can help stimulate the subconscious mind along the right channel. Can you, for instance, realistically associate iron with, say, love and beauty? Of course not. Iron (in one of its forms) reminds us of the weapons of war, these being Martian in nature. Similarly, the color red helps us attune to that energy represented by the planet Mars.

Like attracts like by association and by stimulating the mind along the right channel. It naturally follows that using ritual items that correspond to a particular planet will assist your magical work in a very scientific way, provided you use the correct correspondences. You will find lists of planetary correspondences throughout this book. These can be used with confidence in all your magical work.

Using Planetary Energies

There are two distinct ways in which planetary correspondences can be used in candle magic. These involve "outer" and "inner" correspondences. Before proceeding with this important stage in your magical work, you should be completely familiar with the previous chapters, especially with the technique of opening the inner temple. This is vital to success, for the inner temple forms the foundation on which you can build a powerful and individual magical system. Up until now, you have generalized and adhered to an open plan of action. Now, you will bring in the idea of planetary energies by attuning your inner temple.

You will use outer correspondences by bringing into your ritual physical objects that suggest the planetary energy being used. Consider a ritual that uses the energy of

Venus. The color green should be used as much as possible, for instance, in the form of green candles, altar cloth, or candle holders, and perhaps an altar symbol consisting of the planetary symbol in green or on a green background. Use your own ideas and a little ingenuity. There is no substitute for personal involvement in magical work. The number seven (7) is also Venusian. If you have enough space (and can afford it!), use seven green candles or mark a single candle to represent 7 in some way, either by scribing seven equally spaced lines from top to bottom or simply by drawing the number 7 itself. You can also use an incense, such as rose, which suggests Venus. The prime magical direction for Venus is North, so place your candle/s at this point on your altar. Should the central candle get in the way, simply move it to some convenient place after lighting it during the initial opening of the temple. Remember, flexibility is the key. If you have to move things around, this is perfectly correct. If there are any gods looking in, they will not mind in the least.

The inner work is, as you now know, done in the mind, in the imagination. With experience, you can manage with very little equipment, but you must always use your imagination in any candle-magic ritual. Failure to do so will inevitably result in failure. Attuning the inner temple is quite simple with a little practice. Having opened your temple (see chapter 3), keep your intention in mind and light your planetary candle/s. Imagine the correct elemental doorway opening and light, in the appropriate planetary color, entering the temple and lighting up the central pool. Impress your intention into the pool using a simple keyword, such as "love," "money," or "better health." See this word on the surface of the pool or imagine that you are writing it in the water with your finger. Use your own ideas and preferences to help personalize the ritual. Now see the pool turn into a fountain of water glowing with the same planetary color. See the temple fill with the same light, which then passes out through the four elemental doorways into the outside world. Pause to contemplate this, not forgetting to be positive and use creative thinking. To close the ritual, see the fountain revert back to a calm pool. See the light disappear, then close the temple as described in chapter 3.

Using the Planetary Correspondences

Your intention dictates the planetary energy you will use. Having decided on this, it is a simple matter to look up the appropriate correspondences and bring these into the ritual.

Suppose that you want to bring abundance into your life. The planet that rules this is Jupiter. The color is blue. This should be worked into the ritual by using an altar cloth, candle/s and, if possible, candle holders in this color. The magical direction is West. The incense is sandalwood or any good-quality Jupiter incense. Gemstones aid concentration. Sapphires are expensive, but much cheaper mineral samples are available. Any blue semiprecious stone will be of value. Place these on the altar in some prominent position. The planetary symbol may be marked or painted on the candles, if you desire. The altar symbol also aids concentration and may be painted on a card or art board, which can then be placed at some convenient point on the altar.

Setting up your altar is largely a matter of choice. Use your own ideas and ingenuity, remembering that the more you get involved, in a personal sense, the better the end result will be. The other useful symbols listed at the beginning of each planet's section can be extremely valuable in helping you personalize your ritual. In this example, you could use a few oak leaves, together with chestnuts, to produce a pleasing decorative effect on your altar, with perhaps some clover blossom in a small vase or bowl. Think about your rituals in this way and do not be afraid to try out new ideas—your ideas!

THE MASTER RITUAL

This is a complete ritual that can serve you well and can be varied according to your needs. The words given are my own. Use them if you wish, or make up your own as you gain experience.

The ritual assumes that you have chosen your intention and that you have organized your temple and altar to suit you. After a suitable period of calmness and relaxation, stand up and approach the altar. Imagine the inner light getting brighter within your heart and say: **"Blessed be my inner, silent center, connecting all, mediating all and encompassing all."**

Light the central altar candle. Imagine the light rising to the upper point of the magic sphere and say: **"Blessed be the crown of creation."**

See the crown in your imagination, then see the light travel to the lower point and say: **"Blessed be the cubic throne of Earth."** See the cube in your imagination.

Imagine a beam of light proceeding toward the East, then see the symbol of a sword and say: **"Blessed be the sword of light, my symbol of the eastern gate."**

Light the eastern candle. Imagine a beam of light traveling toward the South, see a wand, and say: **"Blessed be the wand of power, my symbol of the southern gate."**

Light the southern candle. See the light reach out toward the West, see a magical cup, and say: **"Blessed be the cup of kindness, my symbol of the western gate."**

Light the western candle. See the light move toward the North, see a magical shield, and say: **"Blessed be the shield of** _____ [Here speak your own name, for it is your shield], **my symbol of the northern gate."**

Light the northern candle. Pause and say: **"From inner silence to outer splendor, be the cosmic rings duly formed."**

Imagine the three cosmic rings forming, as directed in chapter 3. Now say: **"I now declare this temple duly opened."**

At this point, you may burn incense and/or relax to quiet music in preparation for the next stage—the opening of the inner temple.

When ready, stand up, look toward the East and imagine that you see the now-familiar yellow doorway of the East. See this open (together with attributes given previously, such as the rising Sun), and say: **"I now declare the eastern gateway open. May the Air energies respond fully to my inner thoughts."**

Do the same with each of the other directions saying:
South: "I now declare the southern gateway open. May the energies of Fire respond to my inner directions."
West: "I now declare the western gateway open. May the Water energies respond to my inner desires."
North: "I now declare the northern gateway open. May the Earth energies respond to my inner motivations."

Focus your attention on the upper point, see the crown, which now has seven jewels set into it. Each one represents a planetary power and is colored accordingly (red for Mars, green for Venus, and so on). Remember with which planet you are dealing and see the appropriate jewel begin to glow with light. Say: **"From the crown of creation, may the power of** _____ [name planet] **flow freely into this temple."**

See the light pour downward, then imagine that it enters the temple through the four elemental gateways, filling the temple with color. State your intention and light a symbolic candle to represent it. Now concentrate on the central pool. See it turn into a fountain of light (the color will, of course, depend on the planet) and say: **"Through the unlimited power of my subconscious mind do I now direct** _____ [name planet] **energy to accomplish my aim, which is to** _____ [state your intention]."** See the light pass out through the four elemental gateways, carrying your intention with it. Direct your attention to the lower point (the cube). See this glow with the same colored light, then say: **"I now declare that** _____ [name planet] **energy has this day found fruition in Earth. From the highest, through the fourfold paths of power, and into being thought has merged with power to produce** _____ [state intention]. **May this, in truth, be so."**

Pause for a while, using creative, positive thinking to see the result actually taking place.

Close the temple by first seeing the pool become calm and then saying: **"Let there be peace within."**

Direct your attention to the upper point, see the crown disappear, and say: **"Let there be peace unto the highest."**

Direct your attention to the lower point, see the cube disappear, and say: **"Let there be peace unto the lowest."**

The planetary candle/s may now be extinguished or, if you desire, may be left to burn—the choice is entirely yours. Direct your attention toward the four elemental points, starting at the East, and say: **"Let there be peace to the East."** See the door close and extinguish the candle.

"Let there be peace to the South." See door close and extinguish candle.

"Let there be peace to the West." See door close and extinguish candle.

"Let there be peace to the North." See door close and extinguish candle.

Finally say: **"Let there be peace all around. I now declare this temple duly closed."**

Extinguish the central candle and leave the temple.

This master ritual will prove to be invaluable if you take the time and trouble to learn and practice it. It is important to remember that no ritual can ever be fully effective if you constantly have to think about what to do next. Good rituals are practiced until they become second nature. Only then can you concentrate fully on the feel of the rite or use the imagination to best effect.

The Power of the Sun

Keywords: Healing, vitality
Symbol: ☉
Color: Yellow or gold
Metal: Gold (gold-colored items may be used)
Magical Number: 6
Scent: Frankincense
Gemstones: Chrysolite, goldstone, diamond
Magical Direction: South

Other Useful Items for Ritual Use: Sunflowers, marigold, bayleaf, any citrus fruits, heliotrope, mistletoe, olives, rice, rosemary, saffron, walnuts

Solar Incense
For dealing with the Sun, healing, and the central self.

Incense No. 1
5 parts frankincense
1 part cinnamon
1 part mace
20 parts sandalwood
A pinch of saffron
A few drops of sandalwood oil

Incense No. 2
4 parts frankincense
2 parts benzoin
1 bay leaf
Marigold flowers for flecks of color
1 cinnamon stick
Benzoin resinoid to moisten

Ritual uses: Gaining confidence, fame, gambling, healing, heart conditions, honor, joy, dealing with officials in high office, organizational abilities, pleasure (all types), popularity, sports, vitality.

You are about to learn the truth about yourself. Within you, within the center of your being, is a vast source of power and abundant goodness. Just as the Sun lies at the center of the solar system, illuminating our planet and giving warmth and sustaining life, so within you is a center that also illuminates and sustains. This center of your being, this inner mind, has the capacity to create whatever you wish by using the abundant power of cosmic life-energy. Your inner mind is limitless. It can and will respond to whatever instructions you care to give it. It cannot, nor will it ever, seek to deny or deprive you. Its sole function is to serve you in every possible way.

Self-confidence comes from accepting this simple truth, from realizing that this inner mind exists, and from learning how to communicate and give instructions to this center of creation. Think about this. How could you be more confident? You are safe in the knowledge that you are in possession of the most potent creative force in the universe. You have this power. Do not dispute it. Do not try to be rational, or to doubt. Just accept this simple truth. Your inner mind has knowledge of everything in existence. It has the capacity to harness the vast reserves of life-energy that pervade the universe at all times—energy that can never be exhausted. By virtue of this connection to all knowledge, to all living things and to the entirety of cosmic energy flow, your inner mind knows no limits or restrictions. Nothing is beyond possibility. It can and will create around you whatever you desire, regardless of what that may be.

Throughout history, those with wisdom and insight have testified to the vast power of the inner mind and have pointed the way: "But rather seek ye the kingdom of God; and all these things shall be added unto you" (Luke 12:31).[1] God, or the kingdom, are not separated from you, nor are they unobtainable. The kingdom of the gods lies within you. It is your inner mind. How can you be separated from part of yourself? How can this be removed from you? It is not possible. Wrong ideas, attitudes of mind, and incorrect beliefs may appear to separate you, but, in truth, you cannot be separated from that which is part of yourself. You have this inner kingdom; you have creative power: "Jesus answered them, Is it not written in your law, I said, Ye are gods?" (John 10:34). Accept this simple truth and let it work for you. Allow it into your mind. God lies within, not in some far distant part of the galaxy, or in some idealistic heaven. The god within is your inner mind, therefore you and God are the same. You have the capacity to create, you are godlike.

If you will only discover the limitless power that you truly have, then you will follow the path of peace leading to inner-mind awareness. Your inner mind will listen. It will advise. It will protect. It will create for you, if you communicate with it—in peace. Only in peace and tranquility will your inner mind be able to assist you. Therefore, let peace into your life and learn the way of tranquil communication with the inner power of your central being. You are at the beginning of an exciting journey—a new phase in your life. You are about to discover your creative power and your ability to control all aspects of your life, by contacting and communicating with the only true source of power—your inner mind. Throughout this book you will be given a truth that will set you free and

---

[1] This, and all following biblical quotes, are from the authorized King James Version of the Bible.

bring abundance into your life. Resolve here and now to practice and meditate regularly on this truth, thereby allowing it to work for you. Remember the word "allow." Allow your inner mind to be simulated by truths. Allow it to work for you. Be patient and allow your life to change for the better through the harnessing of peaceful communication with your inner mind. When you do, opportunities for advancement will occur in natural ways and you will know the truth of inner-mind power.

Every color of magic is available to you through the use of your inner mind and the inner temple, and each color equates to pure energy of a particular type.

Gold: The power of the Sun, bringing self-realization and inner power;

Silver: The power of the Moon, bringing the ability to respond favorably to life-energies;

Orange: The power of Mercury, calming the mind and giving intelligence, alertness, and adaptability;

Green: The power of Venus, bringing the ability to attract material things, to have peace, harmony, and better relationships with others;

Red: The power of Mars, bringing vitality, power, strength, and courage;

Blue: The power of Jupiter, bringing abundance, wealth, joy, and opportunity;

Black: The power of Saturn, bringing patience, endurance, stability, and solid material gain;

White: Pure dazzling white light, bringing realization, intuition, insight, and power itself.

All these colors and more are available, giving their power to you. Accept this power. Allow it into your life. It is yours; it cannot be denied you. In the secret chamber of your inner mind, in your inner kingdom, you are brought into contact with reality and the vast power at your disposal. You may visit this place at any time, for it is given to you freely. It belongs to you. Remember the truth: peace equals power. When you are peaceful, when you direct your mind toward this inner kingdom, power is given to you—power that can be used to better your life in numerous ways. Gradually, you will learn how to enter this inner kingdom easily, by becoming calm, by using your imagination. I am your guide; I will help. Each visit to your inner temple puts you in contact with your inner mind; each visit puts you in contact with power. Gradually, you will succeed. Practice regularly, even in times of stress or when facing problems. Become calm and, in your imagination, visit this place. Stand before the central pool and ask for help, ask for answers. Expect answers and solutions to arrive quickly in natural ways —they will! If you were asking an all-seeing, all-powerful, totally beneficent god for help, you would naturally expect results. Your inner mind is that god, so why should it fail to help? It will never fail, if you ask.

Things to Do

1. Read this section through several times and absorb its ideas fully.
2. Practice the ritual techniques carefully, until you are fully conversant with the correct procedures.
3. Get to know the planets and their correspondences in this and succeeding sections, so that can you not only perform a planetary ritual properly, but will know which planet to use in any given situation. If you are uncertain of which planet to use, simply write to me in care of the publisher, giving brief details and I will advise.

The Power of the Moon

Keywords: Home, imagination
Symbol: ☽
Color: Silver (silver-colored items may be used)
Metal: Silver
Magical Number: 9
Scent: Jasmine
Gemstone: Moonstone, pearl, mother-of-pearl.
Magical Direction: West

Other Useful Items for Ritual Use: Daisies, docks, water, iris, lilies, mirrors, pumpkins, wallflowers

Lunar Incense

I have given three lunar incenses, one each for the Maiden, the Mother, and the Hag (Green Willow, the Silver Lady, and the Hecate).[2]

Incense No. 1: For the Moon Maiden or the Green Willow (New Moon)

2 pounds white willow bark
   (freshly cut and chopped)
A teaspoon of menthol
4 ozs gum myrrh
1 teaspoon oil of jasmine
1 teaspoon violet oil
A little orris root

Mix well and store for several months.

---

[2] Also known as the Triple Moon Goddess, the Great Goddess archetype. Her three faces are sometimes referred to as the Maiden, the Mother, and the Crone.

Incense No. 2: For the Silver Lady, the Mother figure (Waxing to Full Moon)

6 ozs fennel
½ cube camphor
4 ozs myrrh
2 ozs frankincense
A pinch of orris
1 teaspoon best jasmine oil
2 ozs crushed fennel seed

Grind together and store for several months.

Incense No. 3: For the dark Mother, the Hydra of mysteries, Hecate (Waning to Dark of the Moon—three days before New Moon)

1 part poppy seed
1 part myrrh
1⅓ part orris root
½ part bitter aloes
A small dash oil of lavender
1 teaspoon oil of violet
Mint leaves
½ pound rosemary
1 part fennel
½ part mandrake
3 parts frankincense

This is ground and can be stored for several months.

Ritual uses: Digestive troubles, discharges, domestic issues, emotional complaints, female disorders, gastric troubles, glandular problems, hypochondria, insomnia, pregnancy, protection, public dealings and public image, rest, romance. The Moon is especially connected with the home and with magic in general, as it rules the imagination.

Since the beginning of time, the Moon has been observed and its effects noted upon Earth. Even today, the magnetic pull of the Moon is recognized. Its effects on the sea and on plant growth are recognized as immediately obvious. Little wonder that the Moon became an essential focal point for the magical works of ancient people. They worshipped the Moon and the Moon appeared to bless their work. Today, it is accepted that the influence of the Moon is restricted to the magnetic pull on Earth's surface. Although this is quite powerful, this is not the only effect that the Moon as such has.

THE MAGIC POTENCY OF THE MOON

Only when you move into the realms of symbolism does the Moon appear to have magical potency. This should always be borne in mind. As a symbolic pointer to cosmic energy flow, the Moon, like the rest of the planets and the Sun, can be used to startling effect. In a birth chart, the Moon indicates how a person will respond to life and its energies. So it is with the Moon itself. Its position in the heavens shows how Earth will respond. To simplify matters the Moon's position is divided into four phases: New Moon, First Quarter, Full Moon, and Last Quarter. In practical terms, the New Moon indicates the beginning of a new cycle. The Full Moon equates to maximum power. The Quarters act as halfway points between the ebb and flow of lunar tides. It is perfectly feasible, and very practical, to use the lunar tides in magical work, provided that common sense replaces the vast amount of dogma that attempts to govern all magical matters.

For instance, cosmic power flows constantly. You can never be out of contact with it, or you would cease to exist. However, within this flow of energy, there are tides. If harnessed, these can be of enormous value. It is possible to calculate these tides with great accuracy. In ancient days, this was done purely by observation of planetary movements against the background of the stars. With the Moon, this was very easy, since it was so close to Earth and readily observable. You can still do this today. The New Moon and its phases are still obvious to the naked eye. Unfortunately this direct observation tended to over-shadow certain facts. While the New Moon most certain-ly heralds the beginning of a new phase of events, this must not be taken too literally or in a personal sense. Un-less the New Moon aspects some planet or other sensitive point in your own birth chart, the effect may well be min-imal. The presumption, therefore, that the New Moon is ideal for all magical work is without foundation. There are too many other considerations.

If you have been basing your magical work on lunar tides and not getting results, this may be why. It is one thing to base your entire magical work on the phases of the Moon; it is another to make use of them sensibly. If you are reasonably skilled in astrology, it becomes easy to see when New Moon aspects occur in your own birth chart. But does this mean that all other New Moons are quite useless? The answer is no! When New Moon's form aspects, these give added impetus to magical work. When they do not form aspects, they are still usable, even though the power is less potent. All that is needed is a lit-tle more willpower. Just as when you launch a boat, you can wait for a high tide and do nothing, or you can push the boat out to sea. All that is needed is a little more ef-fort. So it is with the lunar tides.

So far, the object of this chapter has been to show you that the New Moon should not be assumed to be all powerful in magical matters. New Moons are useful, but are not as dominant as people may believe. So why bother with lunar tides in the first place? Because, if used properly and understood fully, they can be harnessed and used to improve many aspects of your magical work. The first step is to remove superstition and unfounded beliefs. The second is to understand the lunar tides. The third is to apply them. These avenues will now be explored in much greater depth.

Here is a very special practical ritual paradigm using the lunar tides as a focal point for solving problems and helping to achieve results. This magical ritual may be used for virtually any purpose, yet requires little in the way of equipment. As with all magical work, it does, however, require some effort in order to gain results. It does not really matter if you are an expert or a complete novice, or whether you have tried before and failed. The principles given will work, if you follow the instructions carefully. Do not rush, take your time, follow the procedure carefully, and understand what you are doing. First, let's look at the theory behind the practical work.

For our practical purposes, the tides of the Moon are most easily accessible, requiring little in the way of esoteric knowledge to harness. This ritual uses the full cycle of the Moon, beginning at New Moon and continuing for approximately twenty-eight days, using each of the phases in turn. The exact time of these phases can be determined quite easily, by looking in any ephemeris.[3]

Unfortunately, there is a great deal of superstition surrounding the lunar tides. This has tended to obscure the reality of these forces. At the time of the New Moon, the Sun and the Moon are conjunct—that is, working together. From a magical point of view, this represents the beginning of a new cycle—a cycle that can be harnessed in a general sense. While it may be important for more knowledgeable practitioners to consider the astrological implications—sign, house position, and the effect

---

[3] You can use Llewellyn's *Daily Planetary Guide, Astrological Calendar,* or *Moon Sign Book.* They all contain a general daily planetary and lunar aspectation. You can also buy *Celestial Influences* calendars, by Jim Maynard (Quicksilver Publications). In England, *Prediction* magazine contains a general planetary and lunar aspectation.

of aspects on their own birth chart—each New Moon and its resulting cycle is still useful.

Practitioners who are familiar with astrology may want to take into account all the relevant astrological implications in order to determine the best potentialities. First, they will consider the sign in which the New Moon occurred, as this will, in effect, modify the lunar energy. For instance, a New Moon in Aries carries different implications, especially on a national level, to a New Moon in Capricorn. Next, they will search for any aspect being formed between the New Moon and the planetary positions in their own birth chart. This is important because each aspect is a channel along which energy may flow. The type of aspect, the planetary aspects, and its house position also give accurate and useful information. These, however, are the finer points of magical work and, without some degree of astrological awareness, they are quite beyond the average worker.

Does this mean that the lunar tides are unusable? Of course not, provided that you use common sense. Look at it this way. You do not have to be a botanist to grow vegetables or roses, nor do you need to become a fully qualified engineer to drive a car. It is all a question of degree. Some wish to study deeply, others do not. So it is with magic.

To pray to the Moon, invoke the lunar goddess, or to seek to cajole power by "drawing down" the Moon with a sword is no answer. While it can be argued that these things get results, it can equally be argued that any sustained thought gets results. Anything you believe will work will get results, up to a point. In magic you use the power of thought in combination with the cosmic tides. It is far better, therefore, to use a realistic attunement to cosmic energies. This saves time and reduces the chance of adopting invalid belief patterns that, sooner or later, begin to clutter the mind, preventing continued success.

The sane way is to use common sense and deal directly with power in its own right. You can do this by following these clearly defined steps:

1. Know what you want. Many rituals fail miserably because of sheer lack of forethought. Remember, it is no use hoping or wishing or being vague. This simply confuses your subconscious mind.
2. Plan your ritual carefully, attending to equipment and other objects.
3. Prior to the ritual, relax and clear your mind of all thoughts of everyday matters, with special accent on removing negative thoughts, such as doubts, uncertainties, and fears.
4. Perform the ritual.
5. Any thoughts concerning the outcome should now be positive. Refuse to have negative thoughts. One of the best ways to move these is to use creative-thinking exercises that envision a positive outcome in the imagination. This helps to keep the channels of power open.

The ritual that follows is based on the lunar tides and their symbolism. It can be used for virtually any purpose. Opening and closing techniques are not discussed, but are being left to the discretion of each individual. For those not fully conversant with such matters, they have been discussed in chapter 3. This ritual works by keeping your mind attuned to your intention over a prolonged, yet precise, period. This is bound to work better than applying only occasional, sporadic effort. Once begun, it must be continued throughout the lunar cycle, not because some inner being will not like it if you stop, but simply because sustained thought gets results, especially if they are linked with accurate and meaningful symbolism.

First, symbolize your intention. One of the best ways to do this is to write it down. There is no need to use runes, Hebrew, Greek, Latin, or strange sigils. There is no substitute for English, or for your own native tongue. This is what you understand, and, if you know what you are saying, your subconscious mind will understand much more easily. Think about what you want; think about it deeply. Then write down a short sentence that epitomizes this. Thinking about it is important. Do not, for instance, simply write down "lots of money." This is too vague and more of a wish than a command. Wishes don't get results; determined positive thoughts do.

Next, symbolize the Moon—remember that a little ingenuity and common sense goes a long way. A plain silver-colored disc made from cardboard is perfectly adequate and will work far better than some little-understood design borrowed from somebody else's grimoire. Understanding is what you need, rather than presumption. All too often, ancient designs are assumed to be magical in their own right. Any piece of equipment is magical only from the point of view of the impact that it has on your mind through your senses. If you really don't understand what you are looking at, your results are going to be poor.

Finally, find some way of symbolizing the lunar tides that you are about to use. By far the best way is to use some sort of altar-top symbol, with the phases of the Moon on it. For instance, draw an Encircled Cross on paper or cardboard. Place this flat on your altar, facing in the correct direction (perfectionists may want to align this with the magnetic poles, although this is not vital). In the center, place a receptacle in which to keep your intention. A small stainless steel ice cream dish will do nicely. A candle can be placed on either side. The lunar symbol should be placed at the eastern point, on the symbol of the New Moon.

There are four rituals to be performed. The first is done at New Moon, the second when the Moon is at its First Quarter, the third at Full Moon, and the fourth on the day of the Last Quarter. Exact times are usually listed in newspapers, or in an astrological calendar or ephemeris. Having determined the right day, plan your ritual and lay out your equipment. All that remains now is to relax into the right frame of mind, taking as long as you need. The more relaxed you are, the better your results will be, due to self-control.

Open your temple in the normal way and burn a suitable incense. Approach your altar and light the right-hand candle, using suitable words to key your mind into the reality behind this. Since this candle represents power, you should, at this point, let your imagination play on the vast potential of cosmic energy at your disposal. Signify this in your words. For instance: "With the lighting of this candle I recognize the vast, eternal, outpouring fullness of cosmic energy that will at all times seek to comply with my desires." You may use whatever words you wish, provided that they embrace the essential idea of limitless power freely available. Then light the left-hand candle, which symbolizes the power of reception— in other words, the ability of Earth to conform to and comply with cosmic energy flow in whatever way you will. Suitable words might be: "With the lighting of this candle do I recognize the willingness of matter to conform to cosmic direction, as willed." Now take the piece of paper on which your intention is written and place it on the eastern point (New Moon), on top of the lunar symbol. Link this to the lunar tides with suitable wording, such as: "At this place and at this point in time, do I align my intention with the lunar tides. Let power flow freely into ultimate fruition." Now sit or stand and make use of the following magical inworld exercise.

You are about to enter your own magical inworld. Do not strain to see mental pictures. You may close your eyes or leave them open, as you prefer. Immediately in front of you is a doorway made of strong English oak. Move toward it in your imagination. Touch it and it opens. Pass through the doorway and find yourself on a path. It is dark. There is no Moon, only the light of the stars. Yet you can see quite clearly. Walk along the path, looking neither to right or left, for, on this journey, you have a definite goal in mind. It seems to get lighter. The Sun is beginning to rise and a new day is about to be born. Now you can see the outline of distant hills as the light gets brighter and brighter. Suddenly, the first golden rays of sunlight burst into view, birds begin to sing, and you can see the sheer beauty of this marvelous land.

Continue along the path, which leads to a gigantic white cube. Nearer and nearer you go, until you are right in front of this vast structure. Look how well this has been constructed—built of pure white stone, yet not a single joint can be seen—a work of utter perfection that seems far beyond the capabilities of mere mortals. The path leads inside the cubic structure, through a great archway. Go through this into the cube. You are now in a vast hall covered in strange symbols of power. The atmosphere is highly charged, and you can feel the energy all round you. You notice that, somehow, this is beneficial and friendly, in an odd sort of way. In the center of the hall is an altar of pure gold. Walk toward it. Laid on the altar is a circular symbol made from silver. As you look more closely, you begin to see that something is written on it. At first, it seems like strange hieroglyphics, but it soon resolves into English. As you look even more closely, you begin to realize that this is your intention. How strange! But wait! Something else is written there. What does it say? "If you seek the power of the Moon, then give the right number and pass through the right door." What number can this possibly be? Which door do you seek? The answer is quite simple. According to tradition, the number of the Moon is nine. What do you do now?

At the side of the altar is a large gong. Pick up the striker and sound the gong nine times. Something strange is happening. The hall is lighting up with a brilliant silver light and the altar has changed into a fountain of sparkling water. How magnificent this is! Now, what was that about a right direction? If you look around the hall, you will see that there are four doorways. Each has a phase of the Moon on it. So it becomes clear. All you have to do is walk toward the doorway that corresponds to the phase of the Moon being used. Of course, you remember which one this is. All that remains is to walk toward it. Pass through the door and discover what lies behind. From now on, you must do this alone. Behind the door, you will find a room in which you will be helped to achieve your goals. I cannot be more precise, for each individual must approach these rooms in his or her own way. Just be natural, ask for help, and spend some time seeing your goal as you would like it to be. If in doubt, just relax and do nothing, bearing in mind that your inner power already knows what you need. [Throughout this period of creative thinking you will find the use of music compatible with water or the Moon very helpful. There are such cassette tapes available and I respectfully suggest you make use of them. These can be played throughout the whole of the ritual.][4]

After a suitable period, it is time to leave. No need to retrace your steps. This is a magical "instate" in which anything is possible. Just turn around to face the door through which you entered this room, pass through it and you are rapidly returned to your own place, in your own time. This is the end of the Moon ritual. All that remains is to close the temple in the normal way, extinguish the candles, then return to normal.

---

[4] For a current tape catalog with ideally suited music write: Valley of the Sun Publishing, Box 38 Malibu, CA 90265. In England, music for relaxation and inspiration is available from New World Press. For a free catalog, write: New World, Paradise Farm, Westhall, Halesworth, Suffolk IP19 8RH England.

Your next ritual is performed when the Moon reaches its First Quarter; this takes about seven days, but it pays to check on the exact time. Naturally, the outer and inner symbolism is changed to suit the occasion. For instance, when the Moon is at First Quarter, the lunar symbol is placed on the southern point of the Encircled Cross diagram and, of course, during the inner journey, the doorway in the inner temple through which you must pass shows the symbol of the crescent Moon. These symbols are shown in figure 4. The remaining two rituals are performed at Full Moon and Last Quarter, with the symbolism again changed to suit the occasion.

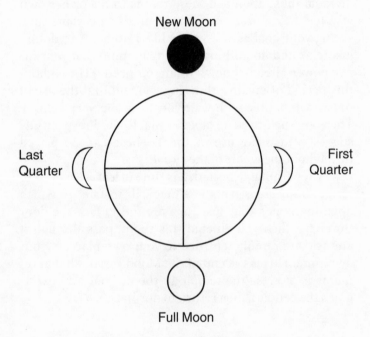

Figure 4. *The Encircled Cross and the phases of the Moon.*

The Power of Mercury

Keywords: Communication, mind
Symbol: ☿
Color: Orange
Metal: Brass
Magical Number: 8
Scent: Storax, lavender
Gemstones: Agate, tiger's eye
Magical Direction: East

Other Useful Items for Ritual Use: Fennel, hazel, horehound, lily of the valley, marjoram, valerian

Mercury Incense
As Mercury is the patron saint, so to speak, of magic, and of visionary avenues, there are many recipes available for incense.

Incense No. 1
1 part gum mastic
1 part cinnamon oil

Incense No. 2
1 part orris root
1 part fennel
1 part pomegranate skin
1 part red sandalwood
A little poppy seed

Incense No. 3
1 part wormwood
1 part flax
A little cardamom
A pinch of anise seed
Camphor
A little chicory

Incense No. 4
1 part valerian root
A little saffron
A little St. John's Wort

Incense No. 5
1 part cloves
1 part frankincense
1 part mastic grains
A little cinquefoil

This incense smells good.

Incense No. 6
1 part violet root
1 part parsley

This incense has an unpleasant smell, but it is very effective.

Ritual uses: Absentmindedness, agreements (loans and contracts), amnesia, anxiety, brothers and sisters, buying and selling, cars, concentration, coughs, education (primary and secondary), headaches, hearing, hygiene, indecision, intellect, interviews, intestinal troubles, knowledge, learning, lungs and lung troubles, memory, neighbors, nerves and nervous complaints, pneumonia, relatives, rumors, slander, speech, stammering, theft, transportation and travel (local), vertigo, worry.

The planet Mercury symbolizes the conscious mind. The god equivalent to Mercury is Hermes, who it should be remembered, is neither male or female. He is androgynous—in other words, a balance of male and female. This, of course, is meant in the best possible sense. There are three paths that lead to the light of realization: the Hermetic or magical path, the Venusian, or Orphic path, and the middle, or mystical path. The Hermetic approach uses the mind, in keeping with the idea of Mercury, the planet of the mind. Unfortunately, most people have a Hermetic bent and tend to get so involved in magical paradigms that they lose sight of reality. They may not see the forest for the trees. Their mental flexibility often becomes academic confusion. The keywords for Mercury are "flexibility," "adaptability," and "communication." These are often missing in modern magic, with its fetish for complication and secrecy.

The training of the mind is an essential part of all real magical work. Positive thinking *must* become a part of your life: as you think—so you are. Positive thinking produces positive results. Negative thinking produces negative results. The major lesson you can learn from Mercury is to reorganize your thinking into more acceptable and realistic patterns. A correctly trained mind can see more clearly. It can evaluate more accurately and is a powerful tool in the right hands. It is a mistake to think that earthly intelligence has anything to do with power. It is one thing to learn so-called facts and become an "intellectual." It is another to become skilled in the use of the mind.

To be a success in this world, you must pass examinations and prove that your mind is capable of great things. Although this may seem like the right approach, in truth, it is not. The true student of the Hermetic arts would not fall for such an obvious mistake. You see, by passing an examination, all that you are really proving is that you have memorized certain facts laid down by the examining body. It is true that you have to exert a certain amount of skill in juggling these facts, but is that any measure of your true skill in using your mind? The answer is no! In the first place, these facts may well be wrong. Witness those students of medicine who were once taught that drilling a hole in a person's head let the Devil out! So much for facts, and for the diplomas that were handed out to those who made use of this information to wipe out perfectly healthy people! Fortunately, the medical profession has now partly dissociated itself from charlatanism of this kind. They have discovered that antibiotics and hygienic surgery actually work. Skill in using the mind revolves around the ability to *think,* rather than absorbing so-called facts and memorizing details. By "thinking," I mean *original thinking.* This is of paramount importance in magic, for the mind must search for and deal with the truth, as opposed to the accepted norm.

To align the inner temple and magic sphere to the power of Mercury is quite simple and follows the paradigms already given in previous chapters. The key lies in using the right symbolism, both outwardly and inwardly, in your imagination. Naturally, the outer symbolism depends on bringing into the temple or place of work all those things that correspond to Mercury. Orange is the correct color. It may be worked into your ritual by using orange altar cloths and orange candles. For those who like to use robes, choose something orange, or perhaps an orange sash or cord with a plain white robe. Jewelry is a matter of taste and personal choice, and may consist of jade or Botswana agate set into brass mounts. Good altar decoration is always useful, provided that it is in keeping with the planet being worked. You need go no further, however, than the four 8s of the tarot deck. These may be laid out on your altar or placed on the appropriate quarter: the VIII of Swords belongs to the East, the VIII of Wands to the South, the VIII of Cups to the West, and the VIII of Pentacles to the North. The Waite deck is far more symbolic than others on sale today. These cards make ideal images for contemplation and meditation. Finally, any good Mercurial incense will serve you well, or you can use storax. Lavender incense sticks also make good alternatives. Your inner symbolism should be clear and precise, and in keeping with reality.

Having collected together all these useful ritual aids, plan out your ritual, open your temple, and imagine before you a doorway. Pass through this door and enter the inner temple of your inner mind. Imagine that right in front of you there is an orange wall that belongs to Mercury. In front of that wall is an altar. Approach this altar and see if there is any message or symbol written on it. Behind the altar, there is another door—this time, with the number 8 written on it. There may be other symbols on it as well. Look to see! Approach this door, open it, pass through it, and explore whatever lies behind. Keep an open mind and allow images and ideas to arise quite naturally. Do not be put off if you do not see masses of imagery glowing in technicolor. Very often it takes time to establish contact with each planetary energy. Remember that, the more you relax, the better this contact will be and the greater the amount of information you will receive.

It is not necessary to go through huge lists of attributions in your mind. The real secrets of the planetary energies reveal themselves when the mind is attuned by intention and is then kept open so that the subconscious mind can then feed back information along the channel that has been created. In this way, you are establishing an uncluttered personal contact with each planetary energy.

The Power of Venus

Keywords: Attraction and love
Symbol: ♀
Color: Green
Metal: Copper (copper-colored items may be used)
Magical Number: 7
Scent: Rose
Gemstones: Emerald, onyx, all green stones
Magical Direction: North

Other Useful Items for Ritual Use: Apple, blackberry, burdock, cherry, coltsfoot, daffodil, elderberry, gooseberry, grape, honey, mint, pansy, pennyroyal, primrose, rose, silk, strawberry, taffeta, vervain, violet, yarrow

Venus Incense

This is a nice Venusian incense to sprinkle over your hot charcoal. It can be used for an intimate dinner for two, as a background perfume in the room with the lights low and your favorite music playing softly. It can be burned ritually, or just for pleasure. This is a traditional incense for Venus. All ingredients are mixed with a little egg white, or the operator's own blood. Since it is traditional, some of its ingredients are hard to find. Use equal portions of each by weight.

Incense No. 1
Musk or synthetic musk crystals
Powdered aloes
Red coral powder
A few drops tincture of ambergris
Rose petals (red)

Here is another Venusian incense of my own:

Incense No. 2
1 cup rose petals
A few drops of ambergris
2 cups sandalwood, finely ground
1 teaspoon synthetic musk
½ cup benzoin
1 teaspoon rose oil
1 teaspoon balsam of Peru
1 teaspoon storax

The last two ingredients are a little hard to get, and may be left out. I mix all my ingredients together, then slowly grind them to a fine powder. Store the mixture for at least a few months. If you can obtain any myrtle wood, it can be rasped into the fine powder.

Incense No. 3
3 parts rose bud
20 parts white sandalwood
5 parts red sandalwood
2 parts rose oil (soluble)
5 parts gum benzoin (preferably Siamese)
5 parts aloe (crushed)
A few drops of musk oil
1 part balsam of Peru
1 part balsam of Tolu

If you wish, add a few drops of your own favorite perfume. Seal the mixture in an airtight box or jar.

Incense No. 4
1 part benzoin
1 part frankincense
1 part cascarilla bark
½ part storax and rose oil

This is a traditional recipe, in contrast to the one above.

Image Wax

If your lover is not "as wax in your hands," here is a wax with which to make an image of him or her. Take 20 parts pure virgin beeswax, 6 parts turpentine, and 2 parts sesame oil. Add coloring as desired, using powdered paint colors. Use this wax as you will, but let the results be on your head. Heat all the ingredients together in a saucepan, gently, being careful not to burn it. Let the mixture cool until you can mold it in your hands. This can be very useful for the relief of rheumatism and as an aid to concentration. Imagine the wax to be a knee joint that is stiff and cold. Warm the wax near the fire and, as the wax image softens, think of the rheumatism going away. You may have other ideas for this wax. I recommend it only for healing!

When you make a wax image that symbolizes your hopes and dreams, you are speaking the eternal cosmic language. It will be recognized and acted upon by subconscious forces when impassioned and lengthy prayers may be totally ignored. A wish expressed in wax symbols is already halfway toward fulfillment, and a coherent image will always produce a material result. This is the whole purpose of image wax—to create symbols of ideas that you are determined to bring into reality.

Your imagination and intelligence enable you to use image wax to help in any practical aim—obtaining a home, a job, an item of luxury, or a social relationship. Apart from helping to achieve material results, it is a most effective instrument in the psychotherapeutic process known as "discovering the True Will." The tranquilizing effect of even quite aimless manipulation of image wax is more marked than that of any of the expensive modern pseudo-magical gimmickry that claims to release tension.

A wax heart can symbolize love or health. Only by using your own wit and imagination will you discover how to make such a symbol apply to a specific situation. You may have to adapt its shape or relative size, or group it with other symbols in a kind of waxen tableau. When you feel that your waxen symbols can be understood at a glance by an alien intelligence, you can be sure that they will produce some kind of subconscious response. Keep your wax symbols in a safe place until your wish is fulfilled. Then melt the wax down and try for another result. An image that has not achieved some response within a month has probably been executed badly. Try again, using alternative symbolism. The important thing is that you alone must think how to express your hopes and wishes in wax. To ask advice is to destroy the magic and ensure failure.

Ritual uses: Affection, association, attraction, companionship, contentment, desires, earning, fiancés, fiancées, finances, financial gains, friends, happiness, income, justice, kidney troubles, leisure, loans, love and love affairs, luxury, marriage, money, ovaries, parties, partners, peace, pleasure, possessions, presents, profit, recreation, relaxation, riches, social affairs, throat troubles, wages.

The keyword attributed to Venus is "victory." This may seem a little strange, but it is one of the delights of magical correspondence that it poses numerous fascinating questions. Finding solutions to these riddles is an integral part of learning the real secrets of the planetary energies, as opposed to either believing totally in the written word or as some do, ignoring these apparent contradictions altogether. There can be no virtue in either of these approaches, even though they are widespread.

Exactly what is meant by "victory"? Does it mean smashing down the opposition, running riot over those who happen to be weaker, or perhaps sitting smugly on some throne of power delighting in the torment of those who have lost? No! This is not what is meant. Ideas like this are not, nor can they ever be, part of the real scheme of life, which teaches only perfection and harmony. Think of the "idea" of victory itself. It conjures up good feelings of achievement and success. What is achieved is of little importance, when compared to the actual feeling that you are victorious. The result is forgotten during this temporary elevation of consciousness. For a few seconds, or even longer, the struggle and even the winning of something becomes subservient to that all-important feeling of victory. Life feels very good.

The word "feel" is the important one here, for feelings, like thoughts, are powerful things. By virtue of their power, they can bring you untold happiness or cast you down into the depths of despair. How often have you heard the phrase: "I have hurt his feelings"? Hurt feelings can often be more painful than an open wound. After all, you can always apply a bandage or treat a cut with antibiotics. But how do you heal someone's feelings? Conversely, when someone is optimistic, full of fun, or in love, he or she is unstoppable. Feelings carry the individual through life with ease. Why? The answer lies, once again, in the old problem of positive versus negative. A positive feeling about some aspect of life is just as powerful as a positive thought. If you feel good, you face life with confidence. If you feel companionship, you are motivated to help, often without concern for your own welfare. If you feel desire, you must have that which you desire. Have you ever tried to "turn off" a longing or a yearning for something or someone? It is virtually impossible. If properly directed on the other hand, this desire is bound to attract into your life that for which you long.

Attraction is what Venus is all about. You must learn the correct use of this potent force, however, and not succumb to sloppy sentimentality and self-indulgence. The power of desire is akin to the power of a magnet. In fact, you will often hear the phrase "personal magnetism" used to describe people who seem to have that "certain something." The problem is that most people tend to believe that they do not have that special quality. Well, nothing could be further from the truth. Just as there is a planet Venus in your birth chart, so you are bound to have some personal magnetism, some ability to attract. All that you need do is realize that this exists and that it is usable.

The problem often stems from the incorrect use of comparison. People are urged to compare themselves to the "ideal" man or woman. Naturally, the comparison is made to look one-sided, so that you appear inferior to the "norm" as defined by those in control. Advertising does this all the time by convincing people that they can look like this ideal if they spend money buying a certain product. Of course, they want to give you the impression that you are inferior unless you buy their product. Your desire to be better is, therefore, manipulated by first showing you that you really are inferior, and then by appealing to your desires. They then give you an easy way out—their product! The whole thing resembles the "carrot and donkey syndrome" in its worst possible guise. To be quite honest, it doesn't matter what you wear or even how you look. What really matters is what you really "are" and what you are sending out in terms of thoughts and feelings. If your thoughts and feelings are negative or confused, a bucketful of expensive scent, or even plastic surgery, is not going to bring you lasting happiness.

You are what you are and the sad story of the human race is that you're largely the product of a comparison between what you really are and what you think and feel you should be. Throughout history, people have been seduced into comparing themselves with something higher. Provided that this is done positively, the results can be beneficial. Often, however, this is not the case. Perhaps the greatest manipulators are those who control religion, for they seek to compare you to some god in the worst possible light. You are convinced to look up to some god, but, naturally, you are told that you are inferior. Worse still—you believe it! Esoterics and magic suffer from the same misconception. To compare yourself with someone—be it god or human—and then try to be exactly like that being is pointless. When you do that, you throw away your individuality. To compare yourself to another person or a god and then to consider yourself inferior is also wrong. To look at noble qualities, to aspire to be godlike, is the only truth worth following. A great teacher once said: "Ye are Gods" (John 10:34). Deep within you, there are godlike qualities that simply need to be reestablished and discovered. A first step in this direction is to put your comparisons in perspective.

Everything that exists around you, here and now, is there only because you willed it into existence using the magical trident of creation: thinking, imagining, and feeling. In Venusian rites you are dealing with feeling and the ability to attract. The real victory of Venus must always be the supreme feeling of the ultimate victory gained over the self. What do I mean by this? I do not mean self-flagellation, self-denigration, or any other form of misery preached by cults and religions. There is nothing to be gained from this, other than self-deception.

In particular, you should be wary of those sects that teach the subjugation of your desires. You cannot do this without causing severe emotional stress.

The victory of Venus is purely one of understanding and using the power of desire or feelings. The first lesson is always one of control. This does not mean living the life of a celibate, or going over the top and indulging in sexual fantasies. There is nothing wrong with sex, but some naive people fall for the antics of con artists or perverts who infest esoteric groups, or they think that every ritual should end in some sort of gang-bang. Whatever these personal fetishes are, I do wish that people would stop trying to tie this kind of behavior to magic. If the gods do exist, they are probably much amused by the antics of the fivefold kiss brigade, or the witch queen long past her prime.[5]

Control means *sensible* control, not subjugation or oppression. Uncontrolled emotion simply burns up power and does little to solve problems. In particular you must be very careful in matters of personal relationships. All too often fired up by the silly ideas presented in "instant" magic books, otherwise sane and sensible people nail themselves to yet another cross of unreality, assuming that they can actually compel someone to love them. One serious look at the word "love" ought to be sufficient to prevent this sort of thing. Love involves freedom, not restriction. You can't make someone love you. It is far better to look at the situation, be realistic, and decide if the matter is really worth all the trouble and heartache. Alternatively, it may well be that the reader is too shy to approach the matter in a direct fashion and is therefore seeking to hide behind the secretive veil of fantasy

---

[5] The kissing of the Devil's behind during the traditional black mass, *oscularum infame* (or kiss of shame).

believing that those who seek to sell pseudo-magical spells for the purpose of 'binding' others to love them are not aware of the facts. You need to overcome your inhibitions instead of buying ready-made love spells, and bolster your self-confidence. Remember the old maxim: "faint heart never won fair maiden."

The truth of life is that, in the same way that you think things into existence, so you attract according to your feelings. The lesson is, therefore, one of refining your feelings, so that your desires become a controlled force rather than a nuisance. Look at life, decide what you want, and think positively about it. Use your imagination to see it happening and put feeling into your thoughts. In other words, focus your desires. It is one thing to tell someone to visualize a favorable outcome; it is another thing altogether to put feeling into those pictures. You must be very careful when using your creative facilities. The more positive you are, the better the result, so it naturally follows that it is quite pointless to spend hours in creative thinking or visualization exercises if you are filled with fears, worries, and uncertainties. These exercises should be done with enjoyment. This is the correct way to use your feelings. Be careful not to let old patterns persist. If you are not enthusiastic, spend some time encouraging yourself to be. If you cannot be bothered, stop and correct the feeling. In so doing, you will not only control your mind, you will take control of those essential feelings.

Negative feelings, such as despair, laziness, and the feeling of inadequacy are simply habits. They can be reversed. The more you practice, the easier it will be to master this. Naturally, the results of your work will improve in proportion to your efforts. Of course, there is far more to Venusian energy than attaining life's benefits. The rule, however, is that, unless you have your life, and in this case your feelings, under control, you are unlikely to penetrate the inner secrets of Venusian power. This applies to all planetary energies. First learn to master the physical lessons. Then, and only then, will you be in a position to elevate your consciousness and understand the reality of the planetary powers. With Venus, the lesson must be victory over the feelings that destroy happiness and peace of mind, and careful study and application of all positive Venusian matters—beauty, art, music, nature, and harmonious relationships with others.

The Power of Mars

Keywords: Energy, drive, daring
Symbol: ♂
Color: Red
Metal: Iron
Magical Number: 5
Scent: Benzoin
Gemstones: Ruby, garnet and all red stones
Magical Direction: South

Other Useful Items for Ritual Use: Aloes, catnip, cayenne pepper, garlic, hawthorn, hyssop, mustard, nettles, onions, pepper, sulphur, tobacco

Mars Incense

Called by some "the great misfortune," Mars is creative and fiery and, like fire, a good servant and a bad master. Mars needs careful handling, otherwise arguments and bad temper can spread like wildfire during and after the rite.

Incense No. 1: Modern Mars
4 parts dragon's blood powdered resin
4 parts rue
1 part peppercorn
1 part ginger
1 pinch of sulphur
1 pinch of magnetized iron filings

Grind up the ingredients and put them in an airtight jar. The peppercorns can sting your eyes and make you sneeze, so, in my formula, I leave them out and replace them with clove oil, ground cloves, and cinnamon. It is no good trying to whip up your emotions if you cannot read the spell or if you sneeze and blow out your five red candles.

Ritual uses: Ambitions, appendicitis, blood pressure, burns, conquest, courage, cuts and bruises, self-defense, dentists, disputes, disturbances, enemies, eruptive diseases, enterprise, feuds, fires, fractures, hernias, inflammations, injuries, malicious attacks, migraines, operations (surgical), opponents, pain, pimples, rashes, scalds, self-confidence, valor, vigor, virility.

The word traditionally associated with Mars is "severity." This is not a particularly apt word, however, because it brings to mind the wrong associations. As pointed out in previous chapters, it is very important that negative concepts be kept out of magical paradigms. "Justice" is another keyword associated with Mars that also suffers from these associations. By far the best way to find suitable keywords for a planet is by looking at it. Again, it is essential to keep out all negative ideas, although with Mars, some of these are far too obvious to ignore. Let's look at Mars in its correct role.

Mars is the energizer among the planets. It is responsible for your inner drive. It gives you strength, endurance, power to get things done, and power to surmount obstacles. Used wisely, it is a power for good; used wrongly, it can lead to conflict. Your Martian problems stem from far back in history, when people literally had to fight for everything. Life was one long battle against the elements, wild animals and even other human beings. The rule was fight or die. There was no alternative. Naturally, the strongest and fittest became the leaders. Moreover, people assumed that the stronger the person, the stronger the tribe. And this was true—up to a point.

Gradually, as people turned to more spiritual matters, a priest caste evolved. This never overcame the deep-rooted idea that people needed to conquer in order to succeed, however. Mars appeared at its worst in Rome, and influenced the Romans who conquered as far north as Britain. The Romans epitomized Martian values and passed these values along to the early church militant. For thousands of years, the negative energies of Mars have been inflicted on people, while being considered socially acceptable. Most societies still rule by fear. Even the legal system testifies to this. Let some vigilante retaliate against crime and the law strikes like the Hammer of Thor. Not against the criminal but against the hero! Hell itself hath no fury like outraged incompetence. However, people are apparently still shocked by it. You cannot train soldiers to kill, give them loaded guns and tell them they must not use them. By the same token, you cannot hold Rome and its successors up as model and then expect people to behave like saints. The mindless violence and vandals of today are the result of a Mars-ridden society, and until the negative aspects of this planet are neutralized, there will simply be more violence and more destruction.

You, as an individual, have a choice. You can neutralize this energy within yourself and learn to master your own Mars energy, or you can simply go on allowing it to work against you. Mars is a powerful tool—a sword that cuts both ways. It can give rise to might or misery. Be honest—which would you rather have? The task starts with self-discipline—and I mean this in the best sense of the word. Self-discipline is a gentle process in which people simply take control of themselves, for the sole reason that they recognize that out-of-control energies can damage themselves and others. This has nothing to do with the gods, who, incidentally, exhibit many negative Martian qualities. It has to do with plain common sense and a realization that through the law of cause and effect, whatever you send out has a habit of coming back. It makes profound sense not to cultivate aggression or any other negative possibilities, for to do so means that you may be paid in kind—not through a punishment for sin, but through the law of cause and effect.

As you think, so you are—that is the law. Cause and effect, summed up quite plainly. Think aggression—receive aggression; think hatred—receive hatred. The lesson should be obvious to everyone, yet society and religions have done their very best to bury it under centuries of dogma, so much so that the average person feels honor-bound to blame everyone and everything for their problems. This only reinforces this misconception. Who can really blame them? They do not know the truth.

If you aspire to control in the slightest degree your life and your negative hang-ups, you must first subdue your own self and the circumstances about you. It follows that to control and direct these impulsive Martian drives of the subconscious and make them shape your future as directed, or perform what other tasks we will, is to control the world we live in and what befalls us. And control these drives we do, whether for well or ill, for whatever we do or think is taken by the subconscious as a signal and command that sets the goals for which it strives. Magic, therefore, begins with self-control, which brings endless rewards to the wise, for as has been observed, "the right thing happens to the happy person." Put otherwise, character is destiny. To most people, the days of the Roman Empire are gone, forgotten and irrelevant to modern existence. But if you think the Roman occupation is over, you will have to think again. I am not referring to museum relics and tourist-trodden paths. In fact, through the combined efforts of education, society, and genetics, the negative aspects of Mars are now so deeply ingrained in our subconscious minds and our culture that they will be extremely difficult to remove.

Magical practitioners face the same problem, no matter how much they may try to be spiritual. The first step in overcoming this is to apply self-discipline and to learn to control bad habits such as anger, hostility, and argumentativeness until you can feel the benefits this brings. Calmness will replace restlessness, and you will find that others are much more obliging and helpful. In addition, you will find that your energy levels will appear to be higher. You will feel stronger in the truest sense of the word.

Next, you must rout out hatred and other deep rifts in your mind. These cause just as many problems, outwardly and inwardly, in the form of tension. In particular, you must discard the bad habit of brooding on supposed hurts. By doing this, you erect pictures in your imagination that can affect your subconscious mind, which, in turn, will seek to bring those images to fruition. Since you are feeding negative ideas into your subconscious, the net result *must* be negative, usually taking the form of difficulties that seem to come from other people, or difficulties that are hard to track down. It is very easy to blame bad luck in this situation or to go on hating, but this is not the answer. The real answer lies in changing your bad habit for a better one—focusing your mind on peace and love. With practice, you will see dramatic results. Moreover, if you take the time and trouble to do this, you will know the truth about phenomena such as "psychic attack," for most of this stems from within rather than from some black magic.

The best keyword for Mars is "energy." The first step for mastering the mysteries of this planetary energy lies in learning how to control your own energies so that they do not damage you or others. The results of mismanaged energies can be seen all around you—in sports fanatics and zealots of all types. People delight in control, especially the wrong kind. To match violence with violence is really no answer, and there is little point in blaming the establishment or anything else. What is needed is self-realization. The more you realize the truth, the more the seed of truth will flourish and wipe away past mistakes, not only in yourself, but in the mass of humanity as well. You, as a magical practitioner, have a responsibility to yourself to cultivate the positive qualities of Mars: initiative, daring, courage, boldness, self-confidence, and well-directed energies. By doing this, you help yourself and others remove many of the self-inflicted miseries emanating from the best-forgotten past.

First learn about self and control your energies. Then, and only then, will you begin to realize the real potential and true might of Mars. Mars represents power through the use of controlled energy. It is a mighty force—a force that you have and are entitled to control. I conclude this brief excursion to Mars with the words of an actor: "May the force be with you."

The Power of Jupiter

Keywords: Expansion, luck, opportunities
Symbol: ♃
Color: Blue
Metal: Tin
Magical Number: 4
Scent: Sandalwood
Gemstone: Sapphire and all blue stones
Magical Direction: West

Other Useful Items for Ritual Use: Asparagus, chestnuts, clover, figs, limes, maple, myrrh, oak, sage, sugar, velvet

Jupiter Incense

Incense No. 1
10 parts sandalwood, finely ground
2 parts gum benzoin
1 part balsam of Tolu
2 parts sandalwood oil
½ part oil of cassia
½ part oil of clove

Add a little saltpetre to the water and mold into cones. Dry in a cool place.

Incense No. 2: A traditional recipe
6 oz crushed sandalwood
1 oz balsam of Tolu
A little mace blade
A little saffron
10 drops oil of cinnamon
½ oz aloes
A few drops musk

4 oz powdered clove
3 drops clove oil
Oil of sandalwood
Oil of allspice (only a drop)

Ritual uses: Affluence, benefactors, commerce, communications (distant and abroad), courts of law, diabetes, higher education, foreign affairs, fortune, hope, humor, investments, judges and juries, law and legal matters, liver troubles, luck, personal esteem, pets, prosperity, refunds, riches, taxation, travel (distant and abroad), voyages, wagers, wealth, winning.

You can work with Jupiter in several ways. Although a planet is said to rule certain well-defined objects and circumstances here on Earth, remember that it does not actually exert an influence. The planet is merely a symbolic representation of a certain type of energy, nothing more. Within the realm of this planet, there are things of this Earth that correspond or "equate" to the essential nature of the energy in question. For instance, Jupiter corresponds to the color blue, the metal tin, and the scent of sandalwood. Jupiter is said to rule these things. But of what possible use is this to us? Quite simply, physical objects, colors, and scents all act as focal points for concentration. For instance, if you combine the previously mentioned items under ritual conditions, they will, with practice and association, help you tune in to the energy pattern associated with Jupiter. By using other correspondences, you can tune in to the energies of other planets.

This is one reason why the copious correspondences given in ancient grimoires are best avoided. First, they are generally inaccurate and tend to be based on personal interpretation and medieval thinking. Second, simplicity is always the best rule. Use a few well-defined and accurate correspondences, then add to these according to your personal experience and realization. In your search for the reality of Jupiter, you must understand the nature of Jupiter. From a practical point of view, Jupiter is the planet of expansion and is therefore associated with opportunity, abundance, luck, and wealth.

It is a common error to believe that wealth is for the few or, even worse, that wealth is somehow harmful and should be avoided. The truth of the matter is that wealth is not only your right, it is also well within your abilities to obtain. Any birth chart is simply a symbolic plan of potentials In that plan, the position and aspects to the planet Jupiter will indicate how you are likely to receive Jupiter benefits and, more important, how you are likely to use this. Remember that the cosmic paradigm is not compulsive. It is ludicrous when astrologers talk about fate, karma, or bad charts. Jupiter simply indicates a potential—the potential to expand in whatever way you will. The only thing likely to prevent success is not the planet, but the way in which you use the energies symbolized by the planet. In short your beliefs control how each of the planetary energies will work for you. In the case of Jupiter, wealth-potential is already yours. If you are not wealthy, if abundance is not flowing into your life, if opportunities seem to pass you by, it is not the fault of the cosmos. Nor are you ill-fated. It is your beliefs that are channeling this energy into the wrong areas. The remedy is simply to change those beliefs for better ones. This is where the paradigms of magic are of value.

One of the simplest of these is the use of creative thinking to impress a new idea into the subconscious mind. Take the idea of wealth. Think about it, then imagine that you have it. What would you do? Where would you go? How would you conduct yourself? These are important questions that need to be answered. Instead of accepting what life appears to give you, use this simple technique to change it. It has the advantage of being easy to use and it requires no equipment whatsoever. If performed regularly in a relaxed state of mind it is bound to get results, because you are speaking to your subconscious mind in a way that it can understand. In addition, you are replacing the habitual beliefs that have so far directed your power into restrictive, rather than expansive, paths. Remember: whatever you believe to be true, comes true. Surely it's time to start believing in something better!

When you enter the realm of pragmatic magic, you attune your mind to the planet Jupiter in order to gain results. The intention of your ritual should be thought out carefully, so that doubts, uncertainties, and other distractions of the mind do not intrude. Next, plan your ritual. Get involved in the procedure. The more you put in, the more you get out! Think about the equipment you will use and remember that each item must be symbolic—in other words, it should represent an idea that is in keeping with the nature of the ritual.

Once you've followed a sensible temple-opening procedure, attune your mind to the energy of Jupiter. Forget about incantations to the gods. Instead, use your imagination to bring correct symbolism to bear on your subconscious levels. This is quite easy to do, although it requires some practice. Jupiter is symbolized by the color blue, so try imagining that bright blue light is flowing into your inner temple through the four elemental gates. Allow this to build up in your imagination, then think positively about your intention. Know what you want and know that, no matter what appears to be happening at the moment, you are going to succeed. Next, see this blue light pour out of your inner temple through the same four gates and into the outside world. Finally, spend some time in creative thinking, actually seeing yourself in possession of what you desire. When you are finished, close down the inner temple. It is always a good idea to back up a ritual with regular sessions of creative thinking, as this helps to keep the channels of power open.

From an esoteric point of view, the exploration of Jupiter should always be an individualistized affair. The reality of Jupiter lies within you, not in the best-forgotten past. It is pointless to try to gain valid information unless you are familiar with the cosmic pattern known as the inner temple. This must come first, because it is the master symbol that unlocks your subconscious mind. It is the subconscious that gives true answers and insight into esoteric matters, not the gods. With esoteric working, the high-point of your ritual occurs when you attune your mind to the planet. This should be followed by meditation. The correct correspondences will also help to focus your mind along the right channels. Some of these have already been given. However, in dealing with this planet, you can also make use of the correspondences of the four gates. By far the best ritual aid is a tarot deck. With Jupiter, use the minor cards that belong to the planet—the four 4s.

The prime magical direction for Jupiter is magical West. The remaining directions are found at the other elemental points, moving in a clockwise direction around the circle. Start by opening the western gate using the IV of Cups as the control symbol. Imagine it placed on a door that then opens. Next, proceed to magical North whose symbol is the IV of Pentacles, then to magical East, represented by the IV of Swords, and, finally, to magical South, corresponding to the IV of Wands. You now have five points of exploration: four at the elemental gates and one at the center. This latter point is the most important.

There are numerous ways to work with this central point. Let your own ideas be your guide. I will, however, mention that each gateway may be explored by contemplating the appropriate card or by using the card as a background for an imaginary journey during which you enter the card and explore the visual scenery depicted therein. The central symbol should be allowed to rise up from your inner mind. Don't adopt the medieval (and therefore restrictive) symbolism of others. Discover your own true central symbol for the planet—a symbol that will develop with you and act as another key to your own inner world.

The Power of Saturn

Keywords: Consolidation, limitation
Symbol: ♄
Color: Black
Metal: Lead
Magical Number: 3
Scent: Musk
Gemstones: Onyx, jet, and all black stones
Magical Direction: North

Other Useful Items for Ritual Use: Barley, beech, black-thorn, cypress, ebony, elm, flint, fossils, holly, ivy, moss, rue, rye, senna, yew

Saturn Incense
The ingredients of Saturn, the dark mother, are unpleasant to the nose, but effective. Asafoetida, for example, smells awful, but banishes beautifully.

Incense No. 1
4 parts myrrh
1 part alkanet root
1 part cypress leaves
1 part juniper berries
Patchouli oil (a few drops)

Ritual uses: Building, business matters, chills, chronic ailments, civil service, colds, debts, delays, depression, dislocations, duties, the elderly, endurance, falls, fears, hair, inhibitions, invalids, land, obstacles, oppression, patience, profession, property, secrets, self-control, skin complaints, tranquillity, warts, work.

Saturn represents pure female potential in the same way that Neptune represents pure male potential.[6] Remember, however, that one complements the other. Male potential is that of "giving out," female potential is that of "taking in." One is positive, the other negative. Here, negative is not used as a derogatory term. It simply means receptive. Male potential would be wasted without the receptive, stabilizing influence of the female principle. The one cannot exist without the other. There is much to be gained from the study of this polarity, a polarity that exists throughout the physical universe.

The physical correspondences of Saturn, that dark planet, are somewhat sinister and off-putting. It is quite true that, in any given situation, people will inevitably see the worst. This is especially true of Saturn. To begin with, Saturn is not the planet of death. Death, which is simply a change of state or transmutation, properly belongs to Pluto. It is morbid religiosity that has caused this strange belief. You can see it even today in the wearing of black, which is the color of Saturn, at funerals or other seemingly sad situations. Church funerals are certainly the ultimate in bad taste and just as certainly give the wrong impression of the meaning of death.

Saturn is the planet of form and form implies restriction. How you view this restriction is another matter. As stated, people will inevitably see the worst. But if there were no restrictions, in the truest sense, everybody

---

[6] Neptune, together with Uranus and Pluto, is used more for esoteric magic—that is, they have more use in an arcane sense than the other planets. This is not to say that these planets have no practical use. They do, but in a more abstract way.

would float off into space! With no gravity, screws and nails would not stay in place, car brakes would not work, in fact, life would be just about impossible. Saturn does have its uses. Restriction is valuable in its purest form. Human-made restriction, however, is another matter. With any pattern of energy, as with any other aspect of life, there is choice. Although it is surely pointless to choose the worst kind of restriction, all too often, this is the case, especially with beliefs. You can choose to believe whatever you wish. The trick is to choose correctly, in the light of reason.

Religion teaches all manner of silly restrictions, none of which are valid. Saturn is often abused in this way. Take the idea of Saturn as a tester for humankind. Why should you be tested for fitness? There is no logical reason for this, unless, that is, you believe in reincarnation or karmic debts. People do believe in these things, even though they do not exist and, worse still, they simply accept these dogmas and the restrictions that they inevitably bring. It is, however, an invalid and completely unnecessary restriction. Saturn, or its images, do not act as testers, for there is nothing to test. In reality, life is ruled by free choice.

In a similar vein Satan is often depicted as an overlord, testing people for their fitness to enter heaven. The church invented Satan. The church also invented heaven. Yet they have imposed so many restrictions on this far-away place that they seem to assume that none shall ever enter there. Satan does not exist, other than as an energy force built through years of sacrifice and adoration in the minds of those who subscribe to this image. For that is all that it is—an image, and a bad one at that. As with all cosmic energies, Saturn energy is neither good nor bad. It simply is, existing as it does according to creative laws and principles. Although it may be fashionable to blame

Saturn for all manner of evil, it is incorrect. The problem lies, not with the energy, but within the minds of people. Put simply, if you believe in the wrong ideals and concepts, the appropriate energy will simply seek to comply with your beliefs. It will not seek to offer a solution or presume to apply rules. Beliefs operate through the ultimate law of free choice. Regardless of whom or what you may later choose to blame, it is your beliefs that shape your circumstances—not planetary power.

Perhaps the greatest problem with Saturn is the effect that negative beliefs can have when focusing the planet's power on life and life situations. As a wise man once said, "There is nought to fear other than fear." Other problems associated with Saturn range from depression and worry, to loneliness. The reality of the matter is that, once these problems are faced and questioned, they can be banished forever. In keeping with the law of nature that states that a true vacuum cannot exist, whatever goes leaves an empty space—a space that can only be filled with truth, in this case, the truth about Saturn power in relationship to life and the individual.

One of the best ways of clearing the mind of these and other misconceptions is to look within the inner temple when it is attuned to Saturn. Adopt truth as a ritual intention and, using the simplest of ritual correspondences, contemplate what Saturn means to you as an individual. For deeper work, meditate on the planet using the guidelines presented earlier, once again, seeking the truth. The truth—that is, the real truth—is worth a thousand volumes of magical philosophy. Moreover, it is much easier to digest. Keep truth in mind. Seek truth within the inner temple and your subconscious mind will provide that truth, simply and without question. This is a far better procedure than following supposed pathworkings and long-winded procedures given in medieval textbooks. Remember: someone else's truth simply will not do; it is not *your* truth. Forget about those endless lists of god-names and other dubious attributions. Instead, seek truth and use simplicity. To aid in your search, use the color black, the symbol of the planet, the scent of musk, and, of course, the tarot. The cards to use are the four 3s. They may be used as meditation symbols, either physically or on imaginary levels, as discussed in previous chapters. From a pragmatic point of view, Saturn rules solidity, stability, ambition, career and business interests, and has a great bearing on land, property, personal security, patience, and, of course, endurance. Such are the positive uses of Saturn.

6
PERFECTING THE ART

In this chapter, we will look at some ways to improve your magical technique. This may be done by removing those things that stand in the way of success and by using additional practices that will help you develop your art to a higher level.

There are many blocks to power; some are obvious—others are not. To begin with, the most powerful part of yourself is your mind. It can also be your worst enemy, if left to its own devices. All serious practitioners must eventually realize that, in order to increase the chances of success and improve the quality of work, they must gain mastery over their minds. By this, I do not simply mean the subconscious mind—I mean the conscious mind as well, for this is where most difficulties start. Valuable though it is, the conscious mind is often the very thing that gets in the way, both before and during a ritual.

NEGATIVE THINKING

In order to develop power, start by looking at the way you think in everyday life. Look at the way in which you deal with life, and, in particular, with its problems. How do you react? Do you give in, assuming that there is no hope?

Do you worry? Do you panic? Do you shy away and bury your head in the sand? In short, are you negative or positive? Remember:

As you THINK—So you ARE.

The type of thinking you generally apply toward life will always dictate what happens next. In other words, if you adopt a negative approach, you can only expect negative results, because your dominant thoughts are biased toward them. The lesson is simply to change your thinking from negative to positive. This requires practice, but it is well worth the effort. Look at yourself constantly to see how you react, and each time you find that you are being negative, stop, remind yourself that your thinking will affect the outcome, then change your approach to be positive. You will find that negative thinking is a habit that has crept into your life. Only by adopting a new and better habit can you be rid of it.

These dominant, negative thoughts are bound to impinge on your magical work, for they are part of you. By gradually ridding yourself of these, your magical work is bound to improve enormously. There are, however, other problems that directly affect your magical work. Some stem from habit, others are more subtle.

FEAR

Fear inevitably finds its way into magical work as a direct result of religious dogma, which has sought to eradicate any individual effort toward self-fulfillment. Sooner or later in magical study, you will meet people who will tell you that the use of magical knowledge for personal ends of any kind is "wrong" or "evil." Do not believe it! Using magical knowledge is no more wrong, in itself, than the use of knowledge about agriculture for farming or the use of knowledge about nutritional values in preparing a healthy, balanced meal.

In fact, the use of magical knowledge to help accomplish personal ends is right! What may be wrong is the study of magic merely to gain power, just as it may be considered wrong to merely accumulate a great store of other tools, such as hammers or screwdrivers without ever putting them to any kind of practical use.

You are acquiring magical knowledge to help you make your life better—and that includes making it better in a material sense. It should be a goal of your magical work to become a maker of your own destiny. In one sense, you always have been the maker of your own destiny, but now—as you become a magical practitioner— you will consciously select goals and set out to accomplish them, and to make these goals part of the purpose of your individual life.

There is only one answer to fear: Throw it out! You cannot expect to be successful if you are afraid of being attacked by psychic entities or fearful of the supposed consequences of daring to enter the hidden mysteries. Fear is a thought pattern, a negative pattern. It makes good results impossible. Learn to apply common sense to your magical work by looking at these fears in the light of reason. If you do, you are bound to realize that these disturbing thoughts are untrue.

DOUBTS

Doubts and uncertainties cloud your vision and, more importantly they confuse your subconscious mind. Be realistic: you cannot, on the one hand, ask your subconscious to do something specific while, on the other hand, telling it that it is impossible! Make no mistake: if you doubt, you immediately cut off any chance of success for the simple reason that you cannot tell your subconscious to adopt two different approaches at the same time. Doubts are negative and, as you now know, negative thinking can only produce negative results. Once more, it is a case of changing your thinking to a more positive mode so that, when you perform your ritual, you believe that you are going to succeed, that you must succeed, that you cannot possibly fail.

Everyone has doubts—especially novices. The best way to overcome them is to be determined to win, no matter what doubts your conscious mind may try to throw up. Stick to your beliefs and refuse to waver, especially if this happens during a rite. Eventually, you will acquire a new and better habit—that of knowing that you cannot fail.

LACK OF TIME

There is ultimately only one real way to learn something, and that is by *doing!* Are you doing the great work? That is the crucial question. If you were here with me, in person, I would ask you the same question. The practice given to you in this book, and the ones you will develop for yourself, are all inner practices. I cannot do them for you. I cannot lead you through them. They are for you to do, and if you do them, you will be successful.

If you are not willing to do your practical work, then you might just as well forget—right now—about studying magic! No mere reading is going to do much for you! No assistance from a teacher is going to do much for you! There really is no progress possible—in any field, much less magical—without work! In fact, you often find ancient writers and teachers—the magicians, the witches, the mystics—all describing the study of magic as *the great work.*

SIMPLICITY—THE KEY TO REAL MAGIC

Most magical practitioners agree that, whatever branch of magic they choose to study, they are confronted with endless complications, confusion, and, inevitably, a great deal of contradiction. In essence, magic is quite simple. It can be made complicated, however, for this appeals to certain minds. But it need not be. Candle magic suffers from the same complexities as any other magical subjects, especially with regard to rituals. The norm is to have numerous rites—one to cover every eventuality or remote possibility. There is, however, a far better way. Try having just *one* ritual that can then be varied, depending on circumstances and individual needs. The foundation for this "master ritual" has already been laid, so we will discuss it now in more detail.

WORDS OF POWER

Until now, you have not introduced the spoken word into your rituals, except for the ritual paradigms I have presented to you. Instead, you have concentrated on basic procedures, in an effort to gain a sensible framework from which you can build a powerful and personal magical system. Just as with candles, incense, altar cloths, and other ritual aids, words are a tool that, if used sensibly, can enhance your magical work a great deal.

As with all else in magic, you must *know* what you are doing (or saying) before you do it. For instance, there really is not much point in speaking the name of some archangel unless you fully understand what that image means on all levels of consciousness. Suppose you were told to say: "O thou great Archangel Michael ...". Without understanding the implications of the name "Michael," that statement would be pointless. It would mean very little. Now, suppose you had spent a great deal of time working with the real attributions connected with this image, and that you did fully understand the meanings behind the name. The result would be a far more effective "speaking." Let me take this one stage further by giving you some of the attributions of this name. The Archangel Michael is a solar figure who also belongs to the Fire element. Already, you have some information that is usable and, more important, relates to your magical sphere. The lesson is simply this: If you are going to speak the names of inner beings, first, realize that these are only images. Second, realize that you must understand these images fully before they can be of use. If you adhere to this advice, you will not go far wrong. The alternative is to grovel to a nonexistent entity in the hope that it may oblige. This can lead you into the trap of unrealistic thinking.[1]

The speaking of words generally requires some consideration, for it is not so much *what* you say, as *how* you say it! Take the simple statement, "I feel good." Now try a simple experiment. Say those words, either aloud or in your mind. All you have done is to repeat a simple statement. No thought went into it. Now, try saying those words with feeling—as though you meant them. Try this several times. Do you feel the difference? Those words are beginning to mean something. Finally, repeat the words slowly and deliberately, again with feeling, but, this time, use your imagination to see yourself "feeling good." Get totally involved in the idea of this good feeling. In other words, act as though the words were true. Believe them to be true. Pretend that, for the duration of the exercise, at least, they are true. Now do you feel the difference? It is another matter altogether to speak words with feeling, imagination, and belief. Those simple words then become words of power.

---

[1] These sorts of images are of a specialized subject and are fully discussed in *Inner Traditions of Magic* by W. G. Gray (York Beach, ME: Samuel Weiser, 1978).

The use of words is entirely up to you. You do not have to use words at all. If you do, however, think about those words carefully. Make certain that they mean something and give them power by using your imagination. This need not be done aloud. It can easily be done in your mind, without a sound being uttered. All that really matters is that the words be spoken with conviction.

WORKING FOR OTHERS

There are many ways to do this magically. Let your ingenuity suggest the best way. Here are a few suggestions and illustrations, along with a few alternative candle-magic paradigms.

There are several ways in which the subject (the other person or desire) may be represented in a ritual. In candle magic, it is best to keep things simple, rather than go to extraordinary lengths. Image candles such as male/female, marriage, and so forth, do have their uses if used intelligently, in the light of common sense. There are easier ways, however, to do the same thing. All you need is a single extra candle that can serve to symbolize the other person or the desire. This may be personalized by writing a person's name or symbol on it—two entwined hearts for love, or a dollar sign for money. Take an ordinary candle, say a few magic words and, *hey presto—* nothing happens! Now, take the same candle and let it represent an idea, a type of energy, or even a person. Already your attitude toward this candle has changed subtly, because you are building a relationship with it. The more you think about what the candle represents, the more you treat it as special, the more valuable it becomes as a focus for your mind. The candle is now symbolic—it is not simply a candle; it represents something else in your mind.

Candle-magic practitioners use (or should use) this technique to great effect. In a typical ritual, a candle may represent a person who is to be healed. Color is often brought into play. The candle may be colored to correspond to the person's birth sign, if you happen to know the date of birth, thereby adding to the visual effect and, of course, helping to personalize the rite. To represent the type of energy being used (in the case of healing, this would be the Sun), a gold candle would be used. Other candles could also be used to represent any other factors involved in the ritual, such as the four elements, or pillars of the inner temple, to signify entry.

For your guidance, here are some useful colors to use for the twelve zodiacal signs:

Aries: Red

Taurus: Orange/red or green

Gemini: Orange

Cancer: Amber or silver

Leo: Yellow or gold

Virgo: Light green

Libra: Green

Scorpio: Turquoise

Sagittarius: Blue

Capricorn: Purple

Aquarius: Violet

Pisces: Crimson

These colors work extremely well.

To add further impetus to the ritual, color can be used in other ways, such as in the choice of altar cloths and robes. In addition, incense may be used and, perhaps, music—provided that this, too, is in keeping with the nature of the ritual. Remember, the whole point of ritual equipment is to help you focus your mind. It may be as simple or as complex as you like, provided that it is first thought about in depth. Learning to construct and perform rituals is not something that is achieved overnight. There is much to be learned, and a great deal of thinking and patient planning is involved. For a ritual to be effective, it has to be the result of correct thinking, sensible techniques, an understanding of cosmic laws, and, above all else, an expression of individual effort. Even the simplest of rituals will work, if the degree of personal involvement and sincerity of performance is high. Rituals should be engineered by *you* in the light of your personal understanding of true magical practices and your personal needs. Let me give you a few examples of how you may do this, using simple ritual paradigms.

The Seven-Knobbed Wishing Candle

Magic predates all spoken and written words. Images and actions are its language. It reads the heart and obeys the true will, no matter what fine words the pen may write or the tongue may speak.

Ask yourself why you wish to cast the spell. You must have a definite purpose in mind. It must be one single purpose, a single reason for casting the spell. The spell must be for only one subject, one thing, one cause, one result, or one intention. You cannot combine several desires or several purposes in one act of magical concentration. It is not feasible to combine several purposes, and thus save time. This very combination of thoughts prevents concentration. There must be only one thought in your mind during spell-casting.

If you were to follow the paradigms given here, you would be so busy concentrating on their rules that there would be no time for concentrating on anything else. So I say to you, especially if you are a beginner, that the best method is the *least* method. There is a magical law that holds that, the more you think of what you are trying to do in relation to your subconscious, the more you interfere with the laws that make the results possible. In other words, the more you are objectively aware of the plans and details of spell-casting, the less chance you have of getting in touch with your subconscious mind. This contact with the subconscious mind is called "attunement."

The proper method of attunement is to stop your objective thinking—and that is the hardest thing for a beginner to do. Have you ever tried to stop thinking?

Chances are that, after you have tried for half a second, you begin to question whether you have stopped thinking. Your mind becomes analytical. You begin to wonder whether you are succeeding. All that is interference. It must end before you can have a proper attunement. You must cease to know who you are, where you are, or why you are—or even that you are, at all. You must lose conscious knowledge of your own existence. You must have only a simple thought and that must be the single thought on which you are casting the spell.

A Basic Spell

After you read these instructions through, forget the rules and follow your own inclinations. Remember that thinking of rules and laws will prevent your success. As soon as you have decided upon your single intention, erect the magic sphere. You will need a seven-knobbed wishing candle in the correct color (for example, green for love, gold or yellow for healing). If you cannot obtain a seven-knobbed wishing candle, use an ordinary candle that has been divided into seven sections. Use a knife to mark these sections. Place the candle on some convenient surface. Use an altar cloth, if you wish, and a little incense. Sit down where it is quiet, and light the seven-knobbed wishing candle, touch the first segment and say "I now call on my never-ending supply of subconscious power to achieve [state intention]." Gaze at the candle, sitting in silence, and draw a mental picture of the thing you wish to have result from your concentration. In other words, visualize clearly, using creative thinking, what you want, then stop thinking of it. Keep in mind the fact that the picture you build should consist of an image of the thing you wish accomplished.

In making this mental picture, imagine that you are an artist about to draw the thing you wish upon a canvas of white, either literally or symbolically. Have the picture develop slowly on the canvas, and in truth, see it! Make it as real as you can. *Stop!* Here is the danger line. It is so hard to stop, yet you must, so that the objective mind can release the picture. It cannot do that as long as you keep working on the picture. Now close your eyes and *think of nothing*—not of yourself, or the person who is to be benefited, or the cosmos, or the world, or the room, or anything else. As you stop thinking and dismiss all thoughts from your mind, you will experience a feeling that all is well, and your desire will be fulfilled. When the candle reaches the first segment, extinguish it and leave the room. Keep this up for seven consecutive workings. Any candle remnants may be buried somewhere, with the same idea in mind.

It will take practice to get into the habit of spell-casting in this way. You must overcome the habit of dwelling too long on the thought on which you are concentrating. Just look at the candle and see what you desire in its flame, then stop thinking about it and gaze at the candle with a blank look, without analyzing or questioning. If you wish health, a favor, love, protection, or anything else, visualize it and then dismiss it from your mind. Sit without thinking for a while—preferably for about five minutes, but even one minute is enough for the mind to communicate your desire—your picture—to your subconscious mind. Then rise from your spell-casting. Give no further thought to the matter, and rest in the confidence that your will will be done. To have doubts or sceptical thoughts in your mind during your concentration or after it will send negative signals to your subconscious mind—doubts that what you wish for will come to you. This doubt interferes with a positive response.

A Love Spell

Before looking at a specific ritual for love and personal happiness, bear in mind these few important points. Take a good honest look at yourself. Are you overweight, scruffy, shoulders drooped, hair in a mess? Have you any pride at all in your appearance? If you do not like yourself, how on earth can you expect anyone else to like you? Lack of self-interest and self-confidence are the biggest factors in anyone's failure to appeal to others. Be yourself and people will, I assure you, like the real, genuine you. Hiding behind a mask, or trying to be someone other than who you are, is guaranteed to cause you trouble. Being yourself is not difficult, once you realize that you need not hide away the real you. Your self-image will determine how you appear to others. Everybody has a certain opinion of themselves. Take a look at your own and then decide if it is really what you want, or only a poor substitute.

This spell is designed to improve your self-image and attract happiness. It will not cost you a fortune, as it uses little equipment. The spell is in two parts and should be performed each day for at least two weeks. For equipment, you will need a small bowl to hold some water. You can use boiled tap water, rainwater, or water from a nearby stream. It is entirely up to you. It is, however, preferable to use water that has not lain stagnant, as in a pool. To make the water more magical, add a few drops of universal fluid accumulator or holy water. You can obtain these from most magical supply stores. You will also need a yellow or gold candle. The fire and water elements are extremely important in magic, and, here, you are going to use them to good effect. First, find a place where you will not be disturbed. If you have to, invent some excuse that will prevent people from walking in on you. Finding somewhere quiet can often be a problem, but a little ingenuity will soon solve it. Place the bowl of water and candle on some convenient flat surface and you are ready to begin.

The aim of this spell is twofold: to get rid of inhibitions and self-limiting ideas, and to allow your real nature to come to the fore, thereby bringing true happiness and the right sort of people into your life. In short, it is the magical equivalent of sweeping away the dust in order to let the light come through.

Spend some time relaxing, as described, then simply imagine that everything that is restricting you and preventing personal happiness and fulfillment is leaving you. No need to concern yourself with what these things are, you simply want to be rid of them. They are of no use, and you will be glad to see them go. Let them go slowly and easily. Imagine that they are entering the water in the bowl, like a black cloud. Spend several minutes doing this. When you feel that you have got rid of these things, light the candle, which is symbolic of the real you. Now spend some time imagining that the light from the candle is also entering the water. See the blackness dissolve and a pleasant gold glow replace it. Next, see the candlelight covering you from head to foot in golden light. Feel confident and alive. See yourself, in your imagination, attracting the right sort of people and the right sort of events into your life. Use your imagination and decide what it is that you really want. Do not tell yourself that something cannot be. Imagine only those things that you really want. Spend some time on this. At the end, extinguish the candle and take the water outside. Pour it on the garden and imagine that all your problems are going away, that they are being taken care of by nature itself. Any candle remnants may be buried somewhere, with the same idea in mind.

This spell is simple but highly effective if done with dedication and conviction. It is up to you. You can sit around and put up with personal problems, or you can give it a try. What have you got to lose? A few minutes a day over the next week or so could make all the difference in your life. At the very least, you will certainly learn many things about yourself.

The second part of the spell is specially for the attraction of a member of the opposite sex—be this for marriage or any other kind of relationship. They say that all is fair in love and war, and so it is often the case that the opposite party needs a little push. Unfair? Perhaps! I will leave you to decide. But bear in mind that it would be a waste of time to try to encourage someone who, deep down, does not wish to oblige.

For this spell, you will need three candles, each of which should be marked in some way to indicate that one is for you, one is for the other person, and one is an attraction candle. A good choice of color would be white or gold for a man, black or silver for a woman, and green for attraction, as this is the color of Venus, who rules matters of love. Divide your green candle into seven sections or, if you are really dedicated to your cause, purchase a seven-knobbed wishing candle. Find somewhere quiet to work and place your three candles on some convenient flat surface. Place the male candle to your right and the female candle to your left, about twelve inches apart. In the middle and slightly to the rear, place the green attraction candle. You now have a symbolic plan of action. The spell itself lasts for seven days.

First, relax as described and, when ready, stand up and light the candle that represents you, then the candle that represents the other person, and finally, the green attraction candle. In your imagination, see an emerald green light spread out like a ball from the central candle until it touches the other two. At the same time, feel strongly that you are being attracted to your subject by unseen, yet perfectly natural, forces. Sit down and use creative thinking to see your desires come true. Do this for as long as you like. If you have finished before the green candle has burned down to the first mark or knob, no matter. Leave the room and return occasionally to see when this happens. When the green candle reaches its mark, extinguish all the candles in the same order in which they were lit. Put them away in a safe place.

On the second day, repeat the procedure, but this time, before starting the spell, move the candles closer together. The whole point is that, on the seventh day, they should be together. At the end of the spell, on day seven, let the candles burn out. Take the residue wax, wrap it up in a piece of cloth, green if possible, and put it away in a safe place for as long as necessary.

Finally, if you wish to increase your powers of attraction, whether for love or, indeed, anything else, copper, or copper with a green stone, is the metal to wear. Other Venusian attracters are coral, jade, moss agate, and, of course, the emerald.

A Money Spell

You will need one candle, a candle holder (or saucer) a box of matches or a disposable lighter, and a clean cloth in which to wrap the candle. A handkerchief or similar article will do for this. You will also need a quiet place to work, where you will not be disturbed. An ordinary candle will do quite well, or, better still, try to get hold of a green one, as you are about to use the energy of the planet Venus. Venus rules attraction and money, in a general sense. The use of the color green will help your mind focus on this particular energy in a way that your subconscious mind will understand. Divide your candle into seven sections. Use a knife to mark them. Alternatively, you may purchase a seven-knobbed wishing candle in the right color. These have the advantage of being made especially for magical work. However, the choice is entirely up to you. The spell lasts for seven consecutive days and should be done each day, without fail, at around the same time. This is important. Persist no matter what the distractions or temptations are. If you cannot sustain the effort at this stage, or make a few sacrifices for something far better, then you are unlikely to succeed.

Place the candle in the holder in some convenient place and have the box of matches near at hand. Sit quietly and become calm, pushing aside all everyday thoughts, especially worries about money. Having already decided on exactly what you want before you started, go over this in your mind to reassert your desires in a positive way. Use a creative thinking exercise, as this is bound to help. When you are ready, stand up and light the candle. Touch the first segment with your finger and say: "I now call upon abundant power and direct my subconscious mind to bring to me that which I desire." You need not say this aloud; you can say it in your mind. But think about the words and try to feel them as you say them. Sit down and, in your imagination, try to see an emerald-green light surrounding you, getting brighter and brighter. Imagine that you are magnetized, like a piece of iron, and that you are attracting money. Imagine money being pulled toward you in ever-increasing amounts. See it emerging through the letter box in thick bundles, or falling from the sky like the leaves from a tree, or like snow.

Spend five or ten minutes using your imagination like this, adding any other ideas to the ones I have given to you. Then imagine the green light going out from you into the world, touching everything and everybody who can possibly help, even though they may be unknown to you. If you are troubled with debts, see the light touching the people or the organizations to whom you owe money. See them responding favorably to you and helping you, instead of making demands. Now leave the room and allow the candle to burn down to the first mark or knob. When this point has been reached, blow out the candle, wrap it up in the cloth, and put it away safely. Repeat this spell six times, once each day. When the candle has finally burned away, take the remaining wax and bury it in the garden or drop it into a stream or river.

In order to keep positive thinking going, I suggest that you spend five or ten minutes each day for the next seven days simply performing another creative thinking exercise. This will help considerably. Simply find a quiet place, relax, and spend about ten minutes imagining that the green light is continuing to do its job and feeling that your personal magnetism is continuing to pull money toward you. Give it time. It would be unreasonable to expect thousands of dollars to fall from heaven in a few hours. Do not lose faith in your inner power. Keep thinking positively and, if you so desire, use the creative thinking process for as long as you like. The more you put into a magical working, the more you will get out.

Those who crave wealth, yet gamble or invest unwisely, become poor. The gods have responded to their actions, which demanded poverty, rather than to their words, which were empty of meaning. Such are the laws of magic. There is a time to sow and a time to reap. This is also the law of magic. An egg needs 21 days to hatch and no impatient fidgeting will produce a chick any sooner. A magical spell or ritual brings a response in its own special time.

If you set an infertile egg or sow a dead seed, do not blame nature for its failure to come to fruition. If the musical instrument you buy will not play the right tune, blame yourself and not the craftsperson who made it. Magic lives in the heart, just as music dwells in the musician rather than the instrument.

A Healing Spell
By now you should have an inner temple that is functional. All that is required is to tune this to the planets, in the same way that you tune a radio receiver. For the purposes of magic, the Sun, which is actually a star, and the Moon, which is a satellite of Earth, are both treated as planets

for convenience. Laying aside complex Cabbalistic theories, you can use two simple aids—planetary glyphs and color. Using the color and symbols can help build a rite that invokes the power of the Sun, which rules healing.

Your workplace should be opened up as usual, up to the point at which you change the pool into a fountain. At this point, impress the symbol of the Sun on the surface of the pool and conjure its power, perhaps like this: "I now call on my never-ending supply of solar power." See the fountain rise high into the air, this time, glowing with golden light. Direct the power as before, seeing golden light enter and pass through each of the doorways. You can work into the ritual anything that is of a solar nature, such as gold or gold-colored objects. If using a talisman, use solar symbols.

Tarot cards may also be used as a "target" to focus power, or as a reusable talisman. In the previous rite, with the water element, you could have used one face card, sometimes called a Court card, to represent yourself and another one for your friend, together with the four 10s. These could be placed on either side of the X of Cups as a focus. In the solar rite, the four 6s can be placed in the appropriate quarters, with the subject's target card in the center.

It is helpful to assign the Court cards to subjects of a certain sex and age:

Pages are usually young people (up to age 21);
Knights are men (21–40);
Queens are women (over 21);
Kings are men (over 40).

For example, if your friend is an 18-year-old Aries, you can use the Page of Wands; if you are a 30-year-old Gemini, you can use the Queen of Swords, and so on.

The Tarot Deck and the Planets*

PLANET	SWORDS	WANDS	CUPS	PENTACLES
Uranus	Ace	Ace	Ace	Ace
Neptune	2	2	2	2
Saturn	3	3	3	3
Jupiter	4	4	4	4
Mars	5	5	5	5
Sun	6	6	6	6
Venus	7	7	7	7
Mercury	8	8	8	8
Moon	9	9	9	9
Earth	10	10	10	10

* I have given the complete lists of correspondences of the tarot deck to the planets, even though Uranus and Neptune have not been discussed because of their more abstract uses.

Now It Is Up to You

It is my sincere desire that you be successful in your magical work and, to this end, I have tried, not only to give you a sensible basis for growth and valid magical techniques, I have also attempted to sweep away the idiotic ideas and superstitions that are often presented as magic. Never forget that magic is the science of using your *mind* and that all equipment and accoutrements are merely to help you focus your mind. From now on, whenever you light a candle in a ritual, it should be done in accordance with the principles given to you in this book.

There is always a choice and that choice is *yours*. The choice is simply one of either accepting fate and other unrealistic dogmas, or accepting the truth that you have power and that you can change your life for the better. Life will always seek to comply with your wishes, so, if you choose the path of letting fate govern your life, it will. If you choose the path of power, this also will come true. Life makes no distinction, for it is your choice that matters. If you choose power through the use of magic, life will assist you in every way, provided that you make the effort, by learning and practicing the principles given in this book. I cannot do this for you, or make this choice. All that I can do is to show you the way. From now on,

IT IS UP TO YOU.

May the power on high assist you,
May the Earth respond to your needs,
May the inner self guide you,
May the portals of reality open for you,
And may your efforts be blessed in
ABUNDANCE.

Bibliography

Buckland, Raymond. *Practical Candleburning Rituals.* St. Paul, MN: Llewellyn, 1970.

Cooper, Phillip. *Basic Magick: A Practical Guide.* York Beach, ME: Samuel Weiser, 1996.

——. *The Magickian: A Study in Effective Magick.* York Beach, ME: Samuel Weiser, 1993.

——. *Secrets of Creative Visualization.* York Beach, ME: Samuel Weiser, 1999.

Cunningham, Scott. *The Magic of Incense, Oils, and Brews.* St. Paul, MN: Llewellyn, 1987.

Dunwich, Gerina. *Candlelight Spells.* Secaucus, NJ: Citadel Press, 1988.

——. *The Magick of Candleburning.* Secaucus, NJ: Citadel Press, 1989.

——. *The Wicca Source Book: A Complete Guide for the Modern Witch.* Secaucus, NJ: Citadel Press, 1996.

Geddes, David and Ronald Grosset. *Astrology & Horoscopes.* New Lanark, Scotland: Geddes & Grosset, 1997.

Gray, W. G. *Inner Traditions of Magic.* York Beach, ME: Samuel Weiser, 1978.

——. *Magical Ritual Methods.* York Beach, ME: Samuel Weiser, 1980.

Heidel, Max. *Simplified Scientific Astrology: A Complete Textbook on the Art of Erecting a Horoscope,* 7th ed. London: L. N. Fowler & Co., 1928.

Hone, Margaret. *The Modern Textbook of Astrology.* London: L. N. Fowler, 1951.

Lee, Dave. *Magical Incenses.* Sheffield, England: Revelation 23 Press, 1992.

Leek, Sybil. *Book of Curses.* Englewood Cliffs, NJ: Prentice-Hall, 1975.

Valiente, Doreen. *Witchcraft for Tomorrow.* London: Robert Hale, 1978

Wylundt. *Wylundt's Book of Incense.* York Beach, ME: Samuel Weiser, 1989.

Index

About the Author

Phillip Cooper has been actively involved in magic for over sixteen years. He has examined the nature of astral projection and altered states of consciousness, along with a study of Hermetic magic. He has written *Basic Magick: A Practical Guide,* and *Secrets of Creative Visualization,* two very popular books also published by Weiser. He makes his home in Northampton, England, with his wife and four children.